SYNC OR SINK

The Automation Mindset for Business Survival

Taiwo Omisogbon

TABLE OF CONTENTS

PREFACE...IV
FOREWORD..VI
INTRODUCTION...VIII

CHAPTER 1: AUTOMATION IS NOT A LUXURY.................... 1

CHAPTER 2: THE COST OF DOING NOTHING..................... 13

CHAPTER 3: BUSTING THE MYTHS................................. 24

CHAPTER 4: THINKING IN SYSTEMS, NOT TOOLS.............. 34

CHAPTER 5: PEOPLE, NOT JUST PROCESSES.................... 45

CHAPTER 6: MEASURING WHAT MATTERS IN AUTOMATION ... 55

CHAPTER 7: FROM PILOT TO SCALE, MAKING AUTOMATION STICK.......... 65

CHAPTER 8: CHOOSING THE RIGHT PROBLEMS TO SOLVE...................... 71

CHAPTER 9: LEADERSHIP IN AN AUTOMATED ENVIRONMENT 77

CHAPTER 10: SUSTAINING THE AUTOMATION MINDSET........................ 86

REVIEWS 98

REFERENCES 100

PREFACE

This book was written out of necessity. In my work as an automation engineer, I have observed a recurring problem across industries, businesses are often slowed down not by lack of innovation or talent, but by operational inefficiencies. These inefficiencies are typically rooted in outdated workflows, fragmented processes, and an overreliance on manual effort. The result is a cycle of repeated errors, avoidable costs, and underperformance that puts long-term sustainability at risk.

The global business environment has changed. The margin for inefficiency has narrowed, and expectations for speed, accuracy, and responsiveness have grown. In this environment, automation is no longer a future consideration, it is a present requirement. Yet, despite its importance, many businesses continue to view automation through a narrow lens. For some, it is perceived as expensive and inaccessible. For others, it is misunderstood as a threat to human labor rather than a tool for organizational resilience and growth.

This book introduces the concept of the "automation mindset"; a way of thinking that prioritizes systems, structure, and strategic automation over reactive decision-making. The automation mindset is not about replacing people with machines. It is about redesigning how work is done so that people can focus on higher-value tasks, reduce errors, and scale more efficiently. It is about aligning operations with business goals in a way that supports long-term adaptability.

Each chapter in this book focuses on a specific dimension of this mindset, from identifying hidden inefficiencies to building automation-ready teams and systems. While technical competence is important, the real value lies in leadership decisions, cross-functional planning, and a willingness to embrace change. Automation is not just about deploying tools, it's about structuring work in a way that supports growth, sustainability, and business continuity.

The content is drawn from real business cases, implementation projects, and operational reviews across sectors such as logistics, manufacturing, digital commerce, and enterprise services. The ideas here are practical, structured, and designed to help leaders transition from survival-based operations to systems that are built on scale.

Automation is no longer optional. Businesses must decide whether they will sync their operations with the speed and complexity of today's market or risk falling behind. This book is a guide for those who choose to lead with systems, not guesswork. It is a guide for those who understand that survival in business today depends not only on what you offer, but on how efficiently and intelligently you deliver it.

The future is not waiting. It is already in motion. And it is only those who are prepared to adapt their thinking and their operations that will remain relevant in the years ahead.

FOREWORD

The current business landscape demands more than product innovation or market awareness; it demands operational intelligence. As organizations across the world adjust to increased complexity, rising customer expectations, and the pressure to do more with less, automation has become a defining factor in long-term business performance. Yet, despite its growing relevance, the conversation around automation often remains shallow, limited to buzzwords, tools, or fear of job loss.

This is where *Sync or Sink* becomes essential.

Taiwo Omisogbon has written a timely and practical guide that shifts the conversation from automation as a technical upgrade to automation as a strategic mindset. His work presents a clear, structured approach to understanding how businesses can move from reactive operations to systems that are built for adaptability, precision, and scale. He doesn't simply advocate for automation; he explains how to think through it, how to implement it meaningfully, and how to make it work within the realities of diverse industries.

The strength of this book lies in its practical application. Taiwo draws from years of experience leading automation initiatives across sectors, and it shows. His insights are grounded in real-world implementation, not just theoretical frameworks. The automation mindset he promotes is not about replacing people, it's about empowering them through systems that reduce redundancy, minimize risk, and increase productivity.

As a professional working closely with business leaders, I have seen how the absence of automation affects growth, consistency, and profitability. I have also seen the transformative power of well-implemented automation, how it can unlock capacity, improve decision-making, and position companies for sustained relevance. Taiwo understands this deeply and communicates it clearly.

This book is more than a read; it is a roadmap. Whether you're an executive leading digital transformation, a manager trying to optimize internal processes, or a founder navigating the early stages of growth, *Sync or Sink* offers tools and mental models that will challenge how you see operations, workflows, and value creation.

In a world where speed, systems, and intelligence define competitive advantage, this book equips readers to make the shift, from fragmented workflows to integrated performance, from effort-heavy management to scalable structure. It is a timely reminder that the way we work must evolve, and that the right mindset can make all the difference.

Read it carefully. Reflect on it honestly. And more importantly, act on it.

INTRODUCTION

Businesses today operate in a radically different environment than they did even five years ago. The pace of change is faster, the expectations are higher, and the margin for inefficiency is significantly lower. Whether you're a startup founder, mid-level manager, or executive in a large corporation, you're already feeling the pressure: deliver more with less, move faster than the competition, and remain agile in the face of constant disruption. In this context, automation is no longer a technical option, it is a strategic necessity.

Despite this reality, many business leaders still view automation through a limited or outdated lens. For some, it is considered a high-cost, tech-heavy initiative reserved for large corporations. For others, it remains synonymous with job losses and workforce reduction. And for many more, it is simply misunderstood treated as a one-time upgrade rather than a long-term shift in how business is done. These perceptions are not only inaccurate; they are dangerous. In a business climate where speed, consistency, and insight define competitiveness, operating without an automation mindset is a liability.

This book is written to challenge those misconceptions and introduce a new way of thinking. What I call the automation mindset is not just about tools or platforms, it's about perspective. It is a way of seeing business operations as interconnected systems rather than isolated tasks. It's about designing workflows that are intentional, intelligent, and adaptable. And it's about aligning technology with business goals in a way that creates stability, scalability, and long-term value.

Throughout this book, we will explore what it means to build and lead with an automation mindset. We'll unpack the real reasons businesses struggle to scale, how automation can solve, not create; operational friction, and why successful implementation starts with mindset before it ever touches code or software. We'll also examine the most common pitfalls, from overengineering to lack of stakeholder alignment, and offer a framework for adopting automation in stages, starting small, learning quickly, and expanding strategically.

The chapters ahead are structured to take you from principle to practice. You will begin by understanding the risks of maintaining manual-heavy systems, and then progress to designing automation-ready operations, managing cultural shifts, and building future-proof systems. The content is based on real industry experiences, implementation projects, and common patterns I've seen while consulting with businesses that are navigating growth, digital transformation, or recovery.

Importantly, this is not a book for technologists alone. While automation often involves technology, its implementation is a business leadership challenge. That means everyone involved in operations, strategy, human resources, finance, and customer service has a role to play. Automation works best when it is cross-functional, not siloed. The businesses that thrive in this era will be those who build systems that learn, adapt, and support people, not those who rely on outdated manual control.

As you move through this book, I encourage you to reflect honestly on your current systems. Ask where your team is losing time. Ask what's repeatable but still being done manually. Ask what decisions could be made faster with better visibility. And most importantly, ask whether your current structure can support the future you're building toward.

Sync or Sink is not a metaphor. It is the reality for every business operating today. You either align your operations with the speed and structure required by today's market or you fall behind. This book exists to help you choose the former, with clarity, confidence, and strategy.

Welcome to the shift.

CHAPTER 1
AUTOMATION IS NOT A LUXURY

The conversation around automation in business is often limited, misunderstood, or dismissed. While some see it as an innovation driver, others interpret it as an expensive, overly technical concept meant for large corporations or tech-heavy industries. But the most critical misunderstanding of automation today is the belief that it is optional. In reality, automation has become central to whether a business can survive the current pace and pressure of the marketplace.

The modern business environment demands precision, speed, and adaptability. Customers expect instant service and personalized experiences, while internal teams are stretched thin with rising expectations and limited resources. In this climate, businesses that continue to rely heavily on manual processes are struggling to keep up. They may not collapse immediately, but cracks begin to show repeated errors, slow delivery, communication breakdowns, and loss of customer trust. These cracks eventually widen, leading to a decline that is difficult to reverse.

Automation is not a future consideration. It is part of the present operating standard. Across sectors, companies are automating tasks not for novelty, but for survival. In logistics, automation drives efficient route planning and real-time inventory tracking. In finance, it powers fraud detection and automates compliance. In retail, it simplifies customer onboarding and improves transaction handling. This shift is not exclusive to global tech giants. Small and medium-sized businesses are also finding that without automation, their ability to deliver consistently and scale sustainably is significantly limited.

One of the most common reasons businesses delay automation is their confidence in existing manual systems. These systems feel familiar, even dependable. They are rooted in processes that teams have followed for years, often built on institutional memory and informal communication. While this may work in the short term, it creates long-term fragility. Manual systems are prone to human error, inefficiency, and inconsistency. They also make it difficult to access accurate, real-time data; data that is essential for making fast, informed decisions in a competitive environment.

Relying on people to remember, repeat, and coordinate every detail of a process without system support is not only inefficient; it is unsustainable. As businesses grow, the complexity of operations increases. Without automation, every new customer, order, or task adds pressure to an already overextended team. What follows is a buildup of operational debt, the cumulative cost of inefficiency, missed opportunities, and resource mismanagement. This debt becomes evident in rising costs, employee burnout, and declining customer satisfaction.

Automation addresses these issues not by replacing people but by creating stability and consistency in operations. It introduces structure where chaos once existed. A well-automated system removes the guesswork from repetitive tasks, ensures accuracy, and allows for better monitoring of performance. The goal is not to eliminate human contribution but to elevate it, freeing up time for strategic thinking, creative problem-solving, and meaningful customer engagement.

When viewed correctly, automation becomes more than a productivity tool. It becomes a foundation for business continuity. It reduces the risk of dependency on specific individuals, ensures that processes continue uninterrupted during times of change, and provides clear visibility into operations. This makes it easier to identify what's working, what's not, and where adjustments are needed.

Automation is also a key driver of scalability. A business that needs to increase output should not be forced to hire additional staff every time it grows. That model becomes expensive and difficult to manage. Automation allows businesses to grow without linearly increasing their cost base. It provides the ability to handle more volume, more data, and more complexity without sacrificing quality or control.

The objection that automation is too costly or complex is increasingly unfounded. Today, a wide range of affordable, user-friendly tools exist for businesses of all sizes. What's missing in most cases is not access to tools but the right mindset. Leaders must stop seeing automation as a technology project and begin to treat it as a core business strategy. This shift begins with a commitment to reducing friction, increasing efficiency, and building systems that are designed to last.

The businesses that weather disruption, economic shifts, and rapid market changes are not necessarily the most innovative or well-funded. They are the ones with strong operational backbones. Automation contributes to that backbone by enabling smoother internal coordination, faster response times, and stronger decision-making based on real-time insight. It builds resilience, not just through efficiency, but through clarity and control.

Failing to automate key processes is no longer just an internal issue, it's a competitive disadvantage. Customers are not patient with delays, employees are frustrated by repetitive work, and stakeholders are looking for evidence that a business can scale without imploding. Every day spent managing the same manual processes is a day spent falling behind competitors who are streamlining, integrating, and adapting.

There is a decision every business must make: to evolve or to remain static. Automation is not a trend; it is the new default. To ignore it is to operate with a significant handicap. To embrace it is to take the first step toward building a business that can survive and thrive, no matter what changes lie ahead.

1.1 Why Waiting Is No Longer an Advantage

There was a time when early adopters of automation held a unique edge. They could reduce costs, move faster, and operate with fewer errors, all while competitors clung to traditional methods. But that edge has quickly shifted from advantage to expectation. Automation is no longer a premium feature of high-performing companies; it is becoming the baseline for survival in a digitized economy.

Waiting used to offer the perceived benefit of observing what others do, learning from their mistakes, and entering the game with fewer risks. That strategy is no longer effective. In today's business environment, the cost of delay outweighs the comfort of observation. Markets are moving too fast, and the gap between automated and non-automated businesses widens each year. What used to be competitive strategy has now become operational necessity.

Many businesses that delayed digital transformation during previous shifts such as the shift to e-commerce or mobile responsiveness found themselves scrambling to catch up when the market demanded change. The same pattern is now happening with automation. Organizations that continue to postpone automation initiatives in the hope of "more stability" or "better timing" will find themselves playing a losing game of catch-up.

The belief that waiting saves money or protects team culture is usually short-lived. As inefficiencies accumulate, so do hidden costs: overtime expenses, client dissatisfaction, missed deadlines, employee fatigue, and an inability to handle increased demand. These costs often go unmeasured, yet they slowly erode the business's ability to grow or compete.

Even worse, waiting too long often forces organizations into reactive implementation; scrambling to automate under pressure, without proper planning, change management, or stakeholder buy-in. Reactive automation tends to be rushed, fragmented, and ultimately ineffective, leading to frustration and skepticism that can delay future improvements.

Proactive automation, on the other hand, allows for measured adoption, proper training, and alignment with organizational goals. Businesses that plan early and start small can grow into their systems, giving their teams time to adapt and their workflows time to stabilize.

The longer a company waits, the more it loses the opportunity to shape its systems deliberately. Automation is not just about what you do, it's about when and how you begin. In a rapidly evolving business environment, the decision to wait is rarely neutral. It is a decision to fall behind.

1.2 Automation Isn't About Complexity, It's About Clarity

One of the most common misconceptions about automation is that it introduces complexity. Many business owners assume that automating processes will make things harder to manage, too technical to control, or too rigid to adapt. This belief is not only inaccurate, but also exactly the opposite of what good automation is meant to achieve.

The core goal of automation is clarity through structure. When implemented correctly, automation simplifies. It creates defined workflows, standard operating procedures, and predictable outcomes. It makes business processes visible, trackable, and repeatable. Where there was once guesswork, there is now a system. Where there was dependency on memory or manual follow-up, there is now consistency.

For example, a sales pipeline managed manually through emails and personal spreadsheets creates confusion. No one is sure where a lead stands, what has been promised, or what needs to happen next. But when automated properly, that same pipeline becomes a clear, centralized system where every deal stage is visible to the team, follow-ups are automatically triggered, and conversion metrics are tracked in real-time.

The clarity automation provides extends beyond just processes; it applies to decision-making as well. With real-time data and consistent reporting, leaders can identify patterns, track performance, and make faster, more accurate decisions. They are no longer relying on scattered information or anecdotal updates but are guided by a system that reflects the actual state of the business.

This clarity also reduces internal stress. Employees no longer need to operate in chaos or uncertainty. They know what to do, when to do it, and how their work connects to the broader goal. It frees them from repetitive administrative tasks and gives them more time to focus on high-impact contributions. This kind of work environment improves morale, reduces burnout, and increases accountability.

Of course, automation done poorly can result in confusion. When systems are selected without proper planning or alignment, they can overcomplicate workflows and frustrate the team. That's why automation should never begin with tools, it should begin with mapping out the process clearly, identifying the goal, and selecting solutions that support that structure.

The fear of complexity often stems from a lack of familiarity. But just as accounting software replaced ledgers and CRM systems replaced Rolodexes, automation is simply the next evolution in how business processes are managed. When viewed this way, it becomes clear that automation is not a burden, it is a path toward operational clarity.

1.3 The Real Job of Automation Is to Support Humans, Not Replace Them

Perhaps the most persistent and damaging narrative around automation is that it exists to replace people. This fear has lingered for decades, reinforced by headlines that pit machines against human workers. But in practice, the most effective automation strategies are the ones that elevate human roles rather than eliminate them.

Automation is not a threat to human potential; it is a response to operational drag. It takes over the tasks that are repetitive, prone to error, or low in strategic value. It allows businesses to reduce time spent on administrative routines such as data entry, reporting, scheduling, and manual tracking and redirect that energy toward deeper, more valuable work.

In modern organizations, teams are expected to produce more with fewer resources. Under these conditions, manually executing every recurring task becomes a drain. People become overworked, reactive, and less creative. Mistakes increase. Strategic thinking disappears under the weight of daily to-dos. Over time, employees begin to disengage, not because they don't care, but because they're stuck in a cycle of operational fatigue.

Automation addresses this issue by creating space for people to think, lead, and innovate. When systems handle the mechanical side of business, employees can focus on exceptions, relationships, and improvements. A customer service agent no longer has to manually collect the same customer details for every call. A finance analyst doesn't have to spend hours compiling reports from scratch. A team lead doesn't have to chase every deadline or track every follow-up task personally.

This shift doesn't reduce the need for people; it changes the nature of their work. It moves teams from task execution to insight generation, from order processing to customer relationship building, from reactive handling to proactive strategy. These are the activities that drive real value. And they are only possible when employees are not buried under manual processes.

Additionally, automation reduces the margin for human error. In sectors where accuracy matters such as finance, healthcare, logistics, and legal services, automated systems ensure that nothing is missed, duplicated, or entered incorrectly. This safeguards both the business and its employees, minimizing the risk of avoidable losses and client dissatisfaction.

When employees see automation as an ally, not a competitor, they become more engaged with their work. They recognize that automation doesn't make them irrelevant. It makes their contributions more focused, more strategic, and more visible. But for this shift to happen, leadership must set the tone. Teams must be involved early, trained properly, and given a clear view of how automation is meant to help them, not replace them.

Automation, at its best, is a partnership between systems and people. The system ensures consistency. The people bring judgment, creativity, empathy, and adaptability. When those two elements work together, businesses thrive.

1.4 Getting Comfortable with Continuous Change

One of the biggest challenges businesses face in adopting automation is not technical, it's cultural. Many teams are accustomed to doing things the way they've always done them. Even when those methods are inefficient, they are familiar. Automation introduces change, and with change often comes resistance. That resistance is not always vocal or confrontational, it can appear as delay, avoidance, or lack of adoption. To build automation into the fabric of an organization, leaders must create a culture where change is not feared but expected.

Automation is not a one-time installation. It is a journey. The tools will evolve, the workflows will adapt, and the business needs will shift. What works today may need to be upgraded tomorrow. This means automation is not just about replacing a manual task with a digital one, it's about adopting a mindset that embraces iteration, learning, and continuous improvement.

In environments where change is resisted, automation efforts often stall. New systems get introduced but never fully adopted. Teams revert to old habits. Progress becomes patchy. To prevent this, leaders must focus as much on communication and collaboration as they do on tools and infrastructure. People need to understand why changes are being made, how their roles are affected, and what support is available to help them succeed within the new system.

It's also important to start small and scale gradually. Many automation projects fail because they try to do too much too soon. Introducing automation in phases allows teams to adapt gradually, troubleshoot issues early, and build trust in the system. Each success reinforces the belief that automation works, and that it can be implemented without chaos or confusion.

Over time, as the organization becomes more comfortable with automation, the appetite for improvement grows. Teams begin identifying opportunities on their own. They become more proactive in refining processes and more willing to experiment with tools that drive efficiency. This is the true mark of an automation mindset not just the use of technology, but the normalization of change.

In today's business climate, agility is non-negotiable. The companies that survive are those that can adjust quickly without losing structure or consistency. Automation supports this by providing a flexible foundation. It ensures that even as goals, tools, and markets evolve, the business has the operational muscle to adapt without disruption.

The sooner organizations stop viewing automation as a project with an endpoint and begin treating it as an evolving part of business strategy, the more resilient and future-ready they become. Automation is not here to settle your business into a fixed routine, it's here to equip you for whatever comes next.

CHAPTER 2
THE COST OF DOING NOTHING

There is a quiet danger that threatens many businesses today. It isn't dramatic. It doesn't always appear in the form of a crisis. In fact, it often feels like things are stable, manageable, even predictable. But behind that surface is a pattern of inaction that accumulates slowly until it becomes a barrier to growth, performance, and sustainability. This is the cost of doing nothing, the cost of maintaining the status quo in a market that is moving forward.

Most businesses don't ignore automation because they disagree with its potential. They ignore it because they don't see the urgency. They believe there's still time. They assume their current processes will hold up just a little longer. They weigh the short-term comfort of keeping things as they are against the perceived disruption of change. And in that hesitation, they create a backlog of inefficiencies that grow silently until they become too costly to ignore.

The cost of doing nothing does not always show up in financial statements. It hides in wasted hours, repeated errors, inconsistent service delivery, staff fatigue, and missed opportunities. It shows up in the customer who didn't return because of a delayed response, in the employee who left because they were tired of repetitive, low-impact work, in the sales lead that slipped through the cracks because no one followed up on time. These are the losses that rarely get calculated, but they are real, and over time, they compound.

Businesses that operate without automation tend to build workflows around individuals rather than systems. This means processes live in people's heads or are buried in spreadsheets and emails. When those individuals are unavailable, on leave, or leave the organization entirely, the process breaks. The business becomes vulnerable to turnover and transition. It spends more time reacting to problems than building long-term systems that prevent them. This leads to a culture of firefighting; solving problems one by one instead of fixing the root cause.

There's also a psychological cost to doing nothing. When teams are stuck in manual, repetitive work, morale drops. Innovation stalls. People spend their energy managing tasks instead of solving problems or thinking strategically. They begin to feel replaceable, disconnected, or stagnant. Over time, even the most capable employees disengage because they don't feel like their time is being used meaningfully. The result is not just operational inefficiency, it's talent loss.

The cost of inaction is also reflected in missed scalability. A business without automation may be able to manage a small volume of transactions or customers. But what happens when demand doubles? Without scalable systems, the only way to handle growth is by adding more people, creating more spreadsheets, and increasing complexity. This approach is expensive, difficult to manage, and unsustainable in the long term. At a certain point, growth becomes a threat instead of a goal.

Automation enables businesses to scale without sacrificing consistency. It creates infrastructure that supports more customers, more data, and more decisions without collapsing under the weight of manual effort. The absence of automation makes every expansion feel like a risk. With automation, growth becomes a structured process, not an uncontrolled surge.

Another cost that is often overlooked is reputational damage. In today's hyper-connected world, customers expect speed, accuracy, and seamless experiences. When a business fails to deliver because its systems are slow or disconnected, it loses more than just that customer, it loses trust. Reviews are posted, competitors are compared, and the business's reputation begins to erode. In many cases, the problem isn't the product or service, it's the process behind it. And customers don't wait for companies to fix internal issues; they move on.

From a leadership perspective, doing nothing sends a message. It communicates to the team that operational improvement is not a priority. It signals that inefficiencies are acceptable as long as things look stable from the outside. Over time, this mindset becomes embedded in the culture. Teams stop looking for ways to improve. They settle into patterns that feel safe but are ultimately unsustainable. Momentum is lost, and with it, the ability to respond quickly to new opportunities or challenges.

It's also important to consider how inaction affects decision-making. Without automation, data is often fragmented or outdated. Leaders are forced to rely on assumptions, incomplete reports, or anecdotal input. This slows down the decision-making process and increases the risk of strategic missteps. In contrast, automated systems provide real-time insights that support faster, more accurate decisions. The gap between the two becomes more significant the larger and more complex the business becomes.

The argument for automation is not rooted in hype. It is grounded in the reality that businesses must either align their systems with the pace of the market or fall behind. The cost of automation may be visible upfront; licensing fees, setup time, training but these are fixed, measurable investments. The cost of doing nothing, however, is unpredictable, ongoing, and often more expensive in the long run.

Every day a business operates without reviewing its workflows, mapping its processes, and identifying what can be automated is a day where value is being left on the table. The most successful companies aren't just those with the best products, they are the ones with the best systems behind those products. They are able to deliver consistently, scale efficiently, and adapt quickly because they have built an infrastructure that supports their ambition.

Inaction creates fragility. It keeps businesses dependent on people instead of systems, memory instead of process, hope instead of clarity. And while this fragility may not be obvious during periods of stability, it becomes painfully visible during periods of stress. When demand spikes, when staff changes, when errors multiply, the business finds itself exposed. By then, fixing the problem is harder, slower, and more expensive than it would have been earlier.

The goal of this chapter is to make one point clear: doing nothing is not neutral. It is a choice that carries hidden consequences. Choosing not to automate is choosing to operate below capacity, to risk preventable errors, and to make growth harder than it needs to be. For any business committed to long-term survival and relevance, inaction is the real disruption, not automation.

The longer an organization waits to review and upgrade its operational processes, the more disconnected its internal systems become. What starts as a few manual steps or workarounds eventually grows into a tangled web of inefficiencies. Departments operate in silos. Teams use separate tools that don't communicate. Data is duplicated or lost in transit. Managers spend more time chasing information than using it. This operational sprawl is not always obvious at first, but it becomes a major constraint when the business reaches a tipping point, whether through growth, crisis, or increased competition.

It is also important to note that automation is not solely about improving internal workflows. It directly impacts how businesses engage with their customers. When a client sends an inquiry and receives a delayed response because the support process is manual, the impression created is that the business is slow or unorganized. When a sales lead has to repeat the same information because the CRM is fragmented or outdated, confidence in the brand is weakened.

Customers don't care what's happening behind the scenes, they judge based on what they experience. Without automation, those experiences are inconsistent, and in today's market, inconsistency is costly.

Businesses that continue to operate manually often create unnecessary dependencies. A process that only one person knows how to complete, a spreadsheet only one department has access to, or a task that must be manually triggered by an individual all create fragile points of failure. When any of these piece's break when the person is unavailable or leaves, when the file gets corrupted, or when the email reminder is missed; the process stops. Productivity stalls, deadlines are missing, and recovery becomes reactive. These moments drain resources and distract them from strategic work. Over time, the cumulative effect of these disruptions becomes difficult to ignore.

There is also a branding cost to doing nothing. A business that still functions manually communicates an outdated message; internally and externally. Internally, it signals to employees that their time is undervalued, their potential underused. Externally, it gives customers the impression that the company is behind the curve. In competitive industries, perception matters. Businesses that adopt automation appear modern, proactive, and invested in improvement. They attract more ambitious talent and build greater trust with their market. Those that resist change risk becoming unattractive to both.

For leadership, the pressure to automate is also about future proofing. A leader's role is not just to manage the present but to prepare the organization for what comes next. Automation equips leaders with the tools to plan better, simulate outcomes, monitor performance, and identify risks before they escalate. Without these tools, leaders are left managing blind spots. Their insights are limited, their responses delayed, and their decisions reactive. Over time, this erodes the credibility of leadership itself.

The resistance to automation often stems from a fear of complexity or disruption. But what is often missed is that avoiding automation doesn't avoid disruption, it only delays it. The longer the delay, the harder the implementation will eventually become unavoidable. Businesses that automate under pressure often do so hastily, without proper planning or support, leading to poor outcomes. Those that start early can do so methodically, with time to test, train, and adapt. The difference in outcomes between proactive and reactive automation is significant, and yet it starts with a simple decision: to begin.

There is also a misconception that automation must be done all at once. This belief keeps many businesses stuck. The truth is that automation can and should begin with small, meaningful changes. A single recurring process can be improved. A communication workflow can be structured. A reporting task can be digitized. These early wins create momentum. They prove that automation doesn't have to be disruptive or overwhelming. Instead, it can be integrated gradually, with measurable benefits at every stage.

When automation is treated as a distant priority, the damage is quiet but persistent. It doesn't announce itself with urgency, but it shows up in reduced output, missed goals, high turnover, and declining morale. Over time, what looks like stability is revealed to be stagnation. And in today's economy, stagnation is just another form of decline. No matter how strong the product or how loyal the customer base, a business that cannot evolve operationally will eventually lose ground to one that can.

Automation is not about rushing toward every new technology. It's about understanding the systems that support your business and asking whether those systems are fit for the future. It's about creating infrastructure that isn't reliant on memory, habit, or individual effort. It's about giving your team the freedom to focus on work that moves the business forward, rather than work that simply holds things together.

The cost of doing nothing isn't loud or dramatic, but it is steady and unforgiving. It accumulates in inefficiencies, erodes competitive advantage, and limits the possibilities of growth. Businesses that act early, plan wisely, and adopt automation with intention are not just investing in technology, they are investing in clarity, resilience, and long-term relevance. The ones that wait are not just delaying a decision; they are choosing to operate at a disadvantage.

2.1 Inaction Weakens Internal Accountability

When businesses fail to take intentional steps toward automation, they also inadvertently weaken internal accountability. Manual processes tend to blur responsibility. Because tasks are often tracked informally, through emails, word of mouth, or shared documents, it becomes difficult to determine where breakdowns occur. Was it the finance team that didn't follow up? Or the operations unit that missed a step? Or a miscommunication somewhere in between?

This lack of clarity breeds a culture where mistakes are passed around, not addressed. People begin to work defensively, doing just enough to avoid blame rather than collaborating toward better outcomes. Accountability becomes a personal burden instead of a structural expectation. This is not because employees are incompetent or unwilling. It is because the systems in place do not clearly define who owns what, when it needs to happen, and what success looks like.

Automation, when done correctly, helps restore that clarity. Tasks are assigned with digital tracking, deadlines are built into workflows, and progress can be monitored in real time. This doesn't create a culture of surveillance; it creates a culture of responsibility. People know what they're accountable for, and they have the tools to stay on track. Leaders, in turn, can support rather than micromanage, because performance data is available without the need for constant check-ins.

The cost of doing nothing in this area is subtle but deep. Without structured workflows, organizations start depending on "heroes", those few employees who hold everything together with memory and personal effort. When those individuals are absent or overwhelmed, performance drops sharply. Over time, this creates bottlenecks and discourages others from stepping up, because the system doesn't support shared ownership. Automation spreads responsibility more evenly, backed by process, not personality.

2.2 Your Competitors Are Already Moving

In any competitive environment, the danger of standing still is not just that your business fails to grow, it's that others are gaining ground while you remain stagnant. Competitors who have embraced automation are not simply working faster, they're working smarter. They are delivering more consistent customer experiences, using data to refine their strategies, and scaling their operations with fewer disruptions. The businesses that hesitate, hoping to catch up later, often find that the gap has grown too wide.

Today's customer is not only comparing their service to direct competitors, but they are also comparing it to every efficient experience they've had. If a customer can track their ride in real time or receive automated delivery updates from an e-commerce platform, they begin to expect similar responsiveness in every service interaction. Businesses that can't meet these expectations lose trust quickly.

This isn't just about tech startups or multinational corporations. Small and mid-sized businesses are also embracing automation, not to compete globally, but to win locally. They are using simple tools to automate inventory management, client engagement, internal approvals, and reporting. These aren't flashy changes, but they are effective. And they add up overtime, resulting in faster response rates, leaner operations, and stronger customer retention.

By the time a non-automated business realizes it's losing customers or struggling to expand, it's often too late to respond quickly. Automation, when implemented early, becomes a source of strategic flexibility. It allows businesses to pivot, adapt, and experiment with less disruption. Competitors with this kind of agility will always have an advantage, not because they have more resources, but because they have fewer operational restraints.

The reality is that automation is no longer a secret strategy. It is part of how serious businesses compete. Falling behind isn't just about slower delivery or missed steps. It's about becoming irrelevant in the eyes of a market that expects better, faster, and smarter every year. The cost of doing nothing, then, is not only internal, but also deeply external. It's the slow, steady loss of positioning, relevance, and trust.

CHAPTER 3
BUSTING THE MYTHS

Much of the hesitation around automation doesn't come from lack of access, resources, or even time, it comes from misunderstanding. There are deeply rooted myths that continue to shape how business owners and managers perceive automation. These myths often go unchallenged, passed around as common knowledge or shared assumptions, and they quietly sabotage progress. In order to adopt an automation mindset, it is necessary to confront these myths directly and replace them with informed, practical thinking.

One of the most widespread misconceptions is that automation is too expensive. For many small and medium-sized businesses, the idea of automating internal processes seems like a luxury only larger companies can afford. This belief ignores the wide range of cost-effective solutions available in the market today. From cloud-based platforms to low-code and no-code tools, automation has become more accessible than ever before. In many cases, the cost of automation is significantly lower than the ongoing cost of inefficiency. The real issue is not the financial burden of automation but the unwillingness to reevaluate existing expenses. Businesses routinely spend more money on manual labor, overtime pay, and error correction than they would on basic workflow automation. The myth of cost is not about affordability; it is about misalignment in priorities.

Another myth is that automation is only for tech-based companies. There's an assumption that unless a business is operating in software, digital services, or high-end manufacturing, it has no real use for automation. This idea is false. Automation is industry-agnostic. Whether it's a law firm automating document reviews, a bakery tracking inventory levels, or a retail store scheduling staff shifts, automation applies wherever processes repeat. The form it takes may vary, but the principle is the same: reduce manual input, improve reliability, and free up time for value-driven tasks. The refusal to explore automation simply because a business doesn't identify as "tech" is a missed opportunity to strengthen its internal structure.

There is also a persistent belief that automation equals job loss. This myth has created a silent resistance within many organizations, especially among staff who fear being replaced. In reality, most automation initiatives are not designed to remove people, they are designed to reassign people to higher-impact roles. Automation takes over repetitive, error-prone work so that human effort can be applied where it matters most. When a business automates its reporting process, it's not eliminating the finance team, it's allowing them to focus on analysis and planning rather than data compilation. When customer support chatbots are introduced, they don't replace agents, they filter basic queries so that human representatives can deal with complex issues. The fear of job loss is often rooted in poor communication and lack of involvement. When teams are informed, trained, and shown how automation enhances rather than threatens their roles, resistance gives way to engagement.

Another common myth is that automation removes flexibility. Some leaders worry that once a process is automated, it becomes rigid and unable to adapt to change. This fear is rooted in a misunderstanding of how automation works. Good automation is not static; it is structured but adaptable. It follows logic that can be modified, rules that can be adjusted, and workflows that can be updated. In fact, automated systems often provide more flexibility than manual ones because they allow for instant updates, real-time tracking, and scalable options. The problem is not with automation itself but with poor implementation. When systems are chosen without proper planning or without considering the unique needs of the organization, rigidity becomes a side effect. But when designed with intent and clarity, automation creates space for experimentation, not confinement.

Some believe automation is too complex to implement without deep technical knowledge. This used to be true, but not anymore. The rise of intuitive platforms, drag-and-drop builders, and plug-and-play integrations has made automation easier to deploy than ever. Business leaders no longer need coding backgrounds to map workflows, set rules, or configure systems. What they do need is clarity on their goals, understanding of their processes, and a willingness to test and learn. Many tools come with guided onboarding, customer support, and templates that simplify the process. Complexity is often a reflection of fear, not actual difficulty. With the right mindset and incremental steps, even the most non-technical team can implement meaningful automation in weeks, not years.

There's also the idea that automation is all or nothing, that if a business can't automate everything, it shouldn't start at all. This all-or-nothing thinking is one of the biggest obstacles to progress. Automation does not need to be comprehensive from the outset. It is perfectly acceptable and often more effective to start small. Automating a single task, such as invoice reminders or onboarding checklists, can save hours of manual effort. These small wins build momentum, reinforce confidence, and uncover new opportunities for improvement. Businesses that succeed with automation don't start big. They start smart. They identify high-impact areas, solve one problem at a time, and grow their systems with experience and insight.

Even among progressive teams, there is sometimes the myth that automation will make the business impersonal. Leaders worry that automating customer communication, internal approvals, or marketing campaigns will create a cold, robotic experience. But automation is not about removing the human touch, it's about amplifying it. By automating routine communication, teams have more time to focus on high-value interactions. A customer who receives a timely, accurate response, even if automated, feels more valued than one who waits days for a manual reply. The personal touch doesn't come from doing everything manually. It comes from being intentional, responsive, and consistent, all of which automation helps enable.

These myths, though varied, have one thing in common: they are built on outdated assumptions. They reflect a version of automation that no longer exists. Today's automation is accessible, flexible, human-centered, and designed to support not replace, modern work. The danger of these myths is not that they exist, but that they go unchallenged. They delay progress, limit creativity, and keep organizations locked in inefficient patterns.

To adopt an automation mindset, these myths must be replaced with better questions. Instead of asking whether automation is affordable, ask what inefficiency is already costing you. Instead of asking whether your industry is tech-focused, ask which processes repeat daily. Instead of fearing job loss, ask how your team's talents could be better used. These questions open the door to transformation, not through hype or overreach, but through clarity and intention.

It's important to understand that myths are not just harmless misunderstandings, they shape behavior. They become internalized in decision-making, influence hiring choices, and even affect how success is measured. When leaders believe automation is too expensive, they underbudget for operational improvement. When teams believe their jobs are at risk, they resist collaboration. When managers believe automation leads to impersonal service, they cling to manual systems that actually damage customer experience through inconsistency.

These beliefs are not benign; their operational liabilities that silently affect performance.

In many organizations, these myths go unspoken but are deeply felt. They are embedded in culture. Teams avoid discussing automation because they've seen failed attempts in the past. They quietly resist changes because their input wasn't considered when tools were introduced. Some departments protect their old ways of working as a form of job security. And over time, these silent myths become stronger than any policy or new initiative.

Breaking these patterns requires more than introducing new tools, it requires resetting the culture. It means having open conversations about what automation actually is, what it's meant to solve, and how it will impact different parts of the business. It means involving the right people early, listening to concerns, and being transparent about goals. Most importantly, it means addressing automation not just as a technology implementation, but as a shift in how the business thinks, works, and grows.

The automation mindset isn't just about identifying the myths, it's about replacing them with truth, clarity, and confidence. When people understand that automation creates room for growth rather than cuts, they become more open to change. When teams see that small automation wins improve daily life, they become more collaborative. When leaders treat automation as a core part of business strategy, not just a side project, they create alignment across departments and set the tone for sustainable transformation.

The myth of complexity, for instance, fades quickly when businesses start with small tools that solve real problems. Something as simple as automating email responses, lead assignment, or invoice tracking can show immediate value. These aren't flashy transformations, but they are practical. They show the team that automation is not out of reach, it's already within grasp. And once a few processes are streamlined, the shift in mindset begins to take hold.

In more mature teams, one of the deeper myths is the belief that the business is already too far gone to adopt automation. They assume their operations are too complex, too unique, or too dependent on legacy systems to make automation work. This defeatist thinking is perhaps the most dangerous myth of all. Every company has legacy processes. Every business has quirks in how it operates. Automation doesn't require perfection, it requires willingness. It doesn't ask for flawless systems, it asks for clarity and commitment to improvement. Believing that it's too late is often just another form of resistance, dressed up as realism.

The truth is that any business; regardless of size, age, or industry, can begin to automate. It starts with understanding your current processes, identifying what's repeatable, and choosing solutions that match your actual needs, not someone else's playbook. It's not about imitating big corporations or adopting tools you don't need. It's about tailoring systems to your operations so your business can run smoother, faster, and smarter.

The final myth to address is that automation is only about speed. While efficiency is one of its most obvious benefits, automation also enhances quality. It reduces human error. It ensures tasks are completed on time. It enables consistency in how your brand is experienced, by customers, partners, and employees. It makes compliance easier and reporting more accurate. These improvements touch every part of the organization. And they all begin with the decision to look beyond the noise, beyond the myths, and to approach automation with clear eyes and a structured plan.

3.1 Leadership Sets the Tone for What Becomes Truth

Every organization, regardless of size or structure, takes its behavioral cues from leadership. This is especially true when introducing change, and automation is no exception. If decision-makers are passive, dismissive, or unclear about automation, the rest of the organization will mirror that attitude. If leaders themselves are trapped in myths, believing automation is too risky, impersonal, or unnecessary, then progress will stall before it ever begins.

Leaders don't just manage strategy; they manage narrative. They shape how people feel about new initiatives. If they introduce automation as a threat, it will be met with anxiety. If they frame it as a strategic evolution, one designed to empower the team and strengthen operations, it will be met with curiosity even optimism. People listen to more than just instructions; they pay attention to the emotion, urgency, and energy behind them.

The role of leadership here is not just technical planning, it is cultural direction. It means naming the myths out loud and addressing them clearly. It means bringing skepticism into the open and turning it into conversation rather than quiet resistance. And it means demonstrating, through action, that automation is not something happening to the business, it's something being led, with intention, by the people who know it best.

Leaders should also set the expectation that automation is an evolving process. It doesn't need to be perfect from day one. It will need adjustments, feedback, and refinement. When this is communicated early, it frees teams from the pressure of getting it right immediately and opens the door for honest feedback and shared ownership.

A leader's responsibility is not to know every tool or process, but to build confidence in the team's ability to learn, test, and adapt together. When leadership sets the tone that myths are being replaced with measured experimentation, automation becomes less intimidating and more achievable.

3.2 Myths Don't Just Delay Automation, They Shape Its Outcome

Even when automation is adopted, lingering myths can still affect how it is implemented. A business may purchase software but never use its full capabilities because the team still fears losing control. A manager might automate a workflow but retain unnecessary manual checkpoints because they don't fully trust the system. A department might underreport problems with a new tool because they assume resistance will be punished, not welcomed.

In these cases, the outcome of automation becomes distorted. Instead of streamlining operations, it adds confusion. Instead of freeing people, it frustrates them. Not because automation doesn't work, but because the mindset surrounding it was never addressed. The tools were implemented, but the culture wasn't prepared.

This is why busting myths is not just a precursor to automation; it's a necessary part of doing it well. Myths influence how automation is planned, how teams are trained, how adoption is measured, and how success is defined. If these myths are left unchecked, automation becomes a surface-level fix; one that creates more friction than it removes.

To get the full benefit of automation, organizations must do the invisible work. They must confront assumptions, correct outdated beliefs, and replace them with shared understanding. This requires humility, communication, and time. But without it, automation efforts risk becoming nothing more than underused software, poorly executed integrations, or demotivated teams.

When myths are replaced with truth, automation becomes not just a technical advantage but a cultural asset. It creates a workplace that values improvement over inertia, clarity over fear, and strategy over assumption. That is the true power of the automation mindset, it doesn't just install systems, it transforms how people think about work.

CHAPTER 4
THINKING IN SYSTEMS, NOT TOOLS

One of the most common mistakes businesses make when approaching automation is to begin with tools instead of systems. The enthusiasm to adopt automation often translates into a rush to buy software, subscribe to platforms, or plug in apps without a clear understanding of what problems are actually being solved. The result is predictable: fragmented processes, poorly integrated systems, and teams overwhelmed by tools they don't fully understand or need. This tool-first mentality not only wastes resources, but it also creates more complexity, exactly the opposite of what automation is meant to achieve.

To build a sustainable automation strategy, businesses must begin by thinking about systems. A system is not just a collection of tools, it is a coordinated set of processes, inputs, outcomes, and roles that function together to achieve a specific goal. In a system, every part serves a purpose, and changes to one element have implications for the others. This kind of thinking forces businesses to look beyond isolated tasks and instead ask how things connect, where value is created, and what dependencies exist across teams.

System thinking requires clarity. Before choosing what to automate, leaders need to understand how work currently flows. Where does it begin? What steps does it go through? Who is involved? Where do delays, errors, or confusion typically happen? Without answering these questions, automation becomes a guessing game. It may improve certain areas temporarily but leave deeper problems untouched. Worse still, it may lock bad processes into place, making them harder to change later.

A tool that automates approvals, for instance, might reduce email volume. But if the underlying process for decision-making is unclear, the automation simply accelerates confusion. A CRM system may help track customer interactions, but if sales and customer service teams have different workflows or duplicate data practices, the system becomes a point of conflict, not clarity. In these cases, tools highlight problems instead of solving them—because the system wasn't designed to support the intended outcomes.

Thinking in systems also improves prioritization. Not every process needs to be automated immediately. When businesses map their systems clearly, they can identify which processes are most repetitive, most prone to error, or most important to the customer experience. These become natural starting points for automation. From there, integration becomes intentional. Tools are selected not based on popularity but based on how well they fit into the structure of the system.

Another key advantage of thinking in systems is that it supports scalability. When automation is layered on top of a well-structured system, growth doesn't introduce chaos—it enhances output. The system is already designed to handle more volume, more users, or more complexity, because it was built with coordination in mind. In contrast, when tools are implemented without systems, every new layer introduces risk. As the business grows, so do the chances of breakdowns, duplication, and miscommunication.

Systems also create visibility. When processes are clearly defined and mapped, leaders can measure performance more accurately. They can identify inefficiencies, track timelines, and make data-driven decisions. Automation becomes a way to support those insights, feeding clean, real-time data into dashboards and reports that help guide strategic planning. Without systems, data collection is inconsistent, reporting is unreliable, and leaders are forced to make decisions based on partial or outdated information.

This system-first approach doesn't mean that tools are unimportant. In fact, the right tools can significantly enhance well-structured systems. But the sequence matters. Tools should serve the system, not define it. Businesses must resist the temptation to chase features, branding, or market trends, and instead focus on how a tool fits into their specific workflows, team capacity, and long-term vision. The most advanced software is useless if it doesn't align with the business's actual needs.

Thinking in systems also demands better collaboration. Departments can no longer operate as independent units selecting their own tools and processes in isolation. Marketing, sales, operations, finance, and HR are part of one system, and automation must reflect that unity. Cross-functional planning becomes essential. It ensures that automation decisions benefit the organization as a whole and that no department is optimizing at the expense of another.

Beyond operations, system thinking fosters cultural alignment. It shifts the mindset from short-term convenience to long-term clarity. Teams begin to see their roles not as isolated functions but as contributors to an interconnected process. This reduces friction, promotes shared language, and builds a culture of mutual accountability. Everyone understands how their work fits into the larger picture, and automation becomes a tool for shared progress rather than personal workload reduction.

In businesses where systems are strong, automation feels seamless. Employees don't fear new tools because they are introduced with purpose and supported with structure. Leaders don't second-guess adoption because they have visibility into impact. Customers don't experience delays or inconsistencies because internal processes are synchronized. These organizations don't just use automation, they leverage it.

Adopting a system-first approach takes time and discipline. It requires mapping, documenting, testing, and communicating. It requires asking hard questions and sometimes slowing down to build foundations before speeding up again. But the reward is long-term clarity. A business that understands its systems is equipped to automate with confidence, scale with control, and grow without losing sight of its core processes.

In the automation journey, the greatest danger is mistaking activity for strategy. Plugging in tools may feel like progress, but without a system to support them, those tools become clutter. Real progress begins when businesses stop thinking in terms of features and start thinking in terms of flow. That shift, from tools to systems is what sets apart businesses that automate in reaction from those that automate by design.

A common but dangerous temptation is to believe that automation can "fix" broken systems. In reality, automation only exposes what already exists, whether good or bad. A poorly defined process, once automated, becomes a fast-moving mess. Instead of solving problems, it replicates them on a scale. Without a system to support automation, errors multiply rather than disappear, and confusion spreads faster instead of being resolved. This is why businesses that skip the step of system mapping often experience friction after implementation. They blame the tool when the real issue lies in the absence of structure.

To avoid this, organizations must begin by studying their own operations with honesty. What processes are most vulnerable to delay? Which tasks are repeated across teams? Where are handoffs most likely to break? What dependencies slow down approvals, responses, or delivery? System thinking encourages these questions because it views work as an interconnected journey, not isolated checkpoints. It sees automation not as a quick fix, but as an enhancer of what is already being done with clarity and intention.

This also introduces the idea of ownership. In a tool-centric mindset, the IT department is expected to lead automation efforts. But in a systems-first approach, every department has a role. Operations defines flow. Finance defines accuracy. HR ensures compliance and clarity in people-facing processes. Marketing and sales collaborate on the buyer journey. Everyone is invested, not because they're being forced to use a new tool, but because the system represents how the business actually runs and how it should improve.

Once these processes are mapped and owned, automation becomes easier to apply with precision. Instead of asking "what software do we need?", the team asks "what part of our system is creating friction and what specific support does it need?" This clarity reduces the pressure to adopt big, expensive tools just for the sake of it. Instead, businesses can build a tech stack that evolves over time, each piece serving a defined function, each integration carefully planned.

There's also a noticeable cultural shift that occurs when teams move from reactive tool use to intentional system design. Meetings become more focused. Internal conversations begin revolving around process and impact rather than complaints and workarounds. Employees begin suggesting improvements because they can now see the system as a whole. When something breaks, it's not just a scramble to fix it; it becomes an opportunity to rethink how it fits into the bigger structure.

This kind of thinking fosters innovation from within, not just from the top down.

System thinking is also vital when managing change. When new goals are introduced, such as entering a new market, onboarding a major client, or navigating compliance requirements, businesses with clear systems adapt faster. They know where to make adjustments, how those changes will ripple across the organization, and what controls are needed to maintain performance. In contrast, tool-driven organizations often find themselves scrambling, adding more subscriptions, rebuilding checklists, and retraining people under pressure, all because their operations weren't built on a flexible foundation.

One overlooked benefit of system thinking is the ability to phase out legacy processes without destabilizing the business. Many organizations continue to carry outdated steps or unnecessary approvals simply because no one has questioned them. When processes are viewed in isolation, these inefficiencies are harder to spot. But when processes are visualized as part of a system, redundancies become more obvious, and opportunities for simplification become clearer. Automation then becomes not just about speeding up what exists but about removing what's no longer needed.

Thinking of systems prepares businesses for scale, not just operationally, but mentally. Teams begin to understand that automation is not about doing more of the same, it's about building a structure that supports evolution. As the business changes, the system can adapt. It can grow in complexity without losing control. It can absorb new tools without overwhelming teams. It can serve more customers without compromising quality. And it can support leadership in making decisions that are grounded in reality, not assumptions.

4.1 Systems Bring Visibility, Tools Only Report What They're Told

One of the most overlooked benefits of system thinking is how it enhances visibility. A structured system allows you to see how the business is functioning in real time, not just in theory, but in operational detail. When workflows are mapped and linked to automation, the flow of work becomes trackable. You can identify where bottlenecks happen, where time is wasted, or where approvals are delayed. This kind of transparency allows for proactive intervention.

By contrast, relying on standalone tools rarely delivers this level of insight. Each tool may offer its own analytics, but those reports are siloed and often surface-level. They don't show how one process affects another. They don't reveal whether internal communication is breaking down between teams. Systems thinking closes those gaps. It builds automation not just to complete tasks, but to surface patterns, identify inefficiencies, and empower leaders to make strategic decisions based on what the business is actually doing, not what it appears to be doing on paper.

This visibility extends to people, too. When a system is in place, it's easier to evaluate team performance, assign ownership, and hold departments accountable without micromanagement. Everyone can see what's working, what's slowing things down, and where support is needed. This transparency reduces blame and increases alignment, creating a healthier, more collaborative culture across the organization.

4.2 Integration Should Follow Process, Not Preference

When automation is approached through the lens of tools first, businesses often fall into the trap of buying popular software and then forcing their processes to fit those tools. This backward approach creates unnecessary friction. It introduces workarounds, reduces adoption, and forces employees to adjust their workflow to suit a product rather than improving the workflow itself. Over time, frustration builds, not because the tool is bad, but because it was never designed to match the way the business truly operates.

Systems thinking flips this. Instead of choosing tools based on features or trends, decisions are made based on process clarity. Integration becomes strategic. A business that understands its workflow can choose tools that match the rhythm, timing, and logic of its operations. Integration is not just about syncing data; it's about aligning systems so that one step flows seamlessly into the next. When this alignment happens, automation becomes invisible. It fades into the background, doing its job quietly and reliably.

A clear system also helps determine which integrations are necessary and which are excessive. Many businesses suffer from tech overload, not because they use too little, but because they use too much without cohesion. Redundancy in platforms, overlapping functionality, and bloated processes often stem from the absence of system thinking. By following process instead of preference, automation remains lean, efficient, and far more valuable to the business as a whole.

4.3 Structure Today Prevents Chaos Tomorrow

The long-term benefits of thinking in systems can't be overstated. When businesses take the time to define, map, and align their processes, they build an infrastructure that can weather change. Whether it's a sudden surge in demand, a shift in regulation, or an internal restructuring, a system-based operation adapts with far less disruption. Because the structure is known, processes can be adjusted. Because the logic is clear, training new team members becomes easier. Because ownership is shared, progress doesn't stall when one person is unavailable.

More importantly, systems protect the business from knowledge loss. Institutional memory, the unspoken knowledge that lives in key people's heads is a risk. When those individuals leave, so does the clarity. But when processes are systematized, that knowledge becomes part of the business, not just its people. It lives in workflows, documentation, dashboards, and automation logic. It becomes transferable. Scalable. Sustainable.

Thinking in systems may not feel urgent in the early stages of growth, but as complexity increases, the absence of structure becomes a serious liability. What could once be managed manually becomes unmanageable. What once worked for five clients now fails at 50. Without a strong foundation, businesses find themselves rebuilding under pressure, spending more time fixing issues than delivering value. But when the structure is built early, automation scales naturally. Growth becomes an outcome of design, not improvisation.

CHAPTER 5
PEOPLE, NOT JUST PROCESSES

For all the focus placed on systems, workflows, and technology, no automation strategy can succeed without one critical element, people. Automation is often discussed in the context of process improvement, cost reduction, and operational efficiency, but its most powerful impact lies in how it shapes human effort. Businesses are not machines. They are living ecosystems made up of individuals whose daily actions, decisions, and interactions drive results. Without intentionally bringing people into the center of automation conversations, the most advanced system will fail to deliver its promise.

In many organizations, automation is introduced without fully involving the people who are expected to use or manage it. Tools are rolled out through top-down decisions, processes are changed with little explanation, and teams are left to adapt in silence. This creates friction, resentment, and ultimately low adoption. Employees feel like automation is being done to them, not with them. They begin to see it as a threat rather than an opportunity. And once resistance takes root, no tool, no matter how intelligent or user-friendly, can succeed.

An automation-first mindset must be complemented by a people-first approach. This means automation should be designed with empathy, rolled out with context, and maintained with collaboration. Employees should not be passive recipients of new systems. They should be partners in shaping how those systems are used. Their input matters not only because it increases buy-in, but because they are the ones closest to the actual work. They know where the real inefficiencies are. They understand the nuances that outsiders often miss. Ignoring that insight results in systems that may look impressive on paper but don't align with reality.

People are also the key to sustainable automation because they bring judgment, creativity, and adaptability, three things no system can replicate fully. Automation can handle tasks, but it cannot understand the context of the way people do. It can process data, but it cannot interpret emotion or nuance. It can follow rules, but it cannot break them for the right reason when flexibility is needed. This is why automation should never be viewed as a substitute for people, it is a support system, a framework that enables them to do their best work without being bogged down by repetitive, mechanical effort.

When people are freed from tasks that drain their energy and attention, they can focus on work that adds meaning and momentum to the business. A customer support agent no longer spending hours on manual ticket sorting can now focus on high-touch conversations that build loyalty. A project manager no longer buried in updates and reminders can now focus on coaching their team, identifying roadblocks, and improving delivery quality. A marketing lead no longer stuck generating reports can now analyze trends and craft better strategies. Automation doesn't just improve the output; it improves the experience of work itself.

But for this shift to happen, organizations must also invest in capability-building. Automation changes the nature of roles. It introduces new interfaces, requires new skills, and calls for a shift in how success is measured. Training cannot be optional. Ongoing support cannot be limited to IT help desks. Teams must be equipped with not just knowledge, but confidence; to explore, to adapt, and to continuously optimize. Businesses that fail to invest in this human transition will find that their automation projects stall, not because the tools are faulty, but because the people were left behind.

Equally important is communication. Transparency reduces fear. When leaders clearly explain why automation is being introduced, what it aims to improve, and how it supports, not threatens, the workforce, trust begins to form. The most successful automation initiatives are those where the message is consistent: automation is not about cutting jobs; it's about enhancing value. People want to be reassured that their skills matter in the future being built. They want to understand where they fit. And when they do, they are more likely to champion the change than resist it.

Recognizing the human element also means acknowledging that change is emotional. Even when automation brings obvious improvements, it still disrupts routine, habits, and sometimes identity.

A person who has always been the go-to for a certain manual task may feel a loss of relevance when that task is automated. It's not enough to celebrate efficiency gains; leaders must also make room for people to adjust emotionally, to feel heard, and to reorient themselves within the evolving system. This requires patience, presence, and a willingness to lead through more than just metrics.

Lastly, automation that doesn't serve people is incomplete. The end-user experience, whether internal staff or external customers should always guide automation design. A workflow that is technically perfect but difficult to use is not a success. A chatbot that can answer questions but frustrates customers is not an asset. A dashboard that tracks everything but tells users nothing they need is not helpful. The people who interact with these systems must feel that the experience is intuitive, empowering, and aligned with their goals. Otherwise, adoption will drop, and the system will lose relevance quickly.

Automation is not just a question of tools or timelines; it is a human change. It touches how people work, how they communicate, how they find meaning in what they do. Businesses that recognize this truth and design automation strategies with people in mind will always be more successful than those who treat it as a purely technical upgrade. Because in the end, it is people not just processes, that keep businesses alive, evolving, and positioned to lead.

5.1 Redefining Roles Without Erasing Identity

One of the most delicate, yet often ignored, aspects of automation is its impact on how employees see themselves within an organization. For many people, their identity at work is tied to what they do, not just why they do it. When automation changes or eliminates a task they've owned for years, it can feel like a loss; not of work, but of value.

This is especially true in roles that have remained consistent for a long time. For example, a team member known as the go-to person for reconciling reports or manually processing requests might suddenly find that their relevance has shifted. Even though the automation frees them from repetitive tasks, the emotional transition can be difficult. They are no longer "the expert" in that area. Their contribution, once visible and respected, becomes invisible because the system now handles it in seconds.

This shift is rarely discussed, yet it affects morale, confidence, and even loyalty. People begin to wonder: "What am I here for now?" If that question goes unanswered, it creates disengagement. The employee shows up, but with less initiative, less ownership, and less motivation to grow. Automation is not the enemy in this scenario; lack of communication and recognition is.

That's why leaders must be intentional about how they manage the emotional side of automation. It's not just about replacing a task; it's about repositioning the person. This means proactively identifying how the employees' skills can be redeployed in more meaningful, strategic ways. It means affirming that their value is not tied to a repetitive process but to their insight, adaptability, and contribution to broader goals. And it means making space for employees to express concerns without fear of judgment or exclusion.

When organizations help people redefine their roles in a way that strengthens, not diminishes, their professional identity, something powerful happens. Confidence returns. Engagement deepens. And rather than resisting automation, employees become active participants in shaping it. They bring ideas, help refine processes, and drive adoption, not because they were told to, but because they feel seen, secure, and significant within the system being built.

5.2 Involve the Team, Don't Just Inform Them

Many automation rollouts fail not because the technology is flawed, but because the people expected to use it weren't brought into the process early enough. Too often, automation is introduced through memos, toolkits, or top-down demos. Decisions are made in boardrooms, and teams are simply informed when the new system is ready to go live. While this may seem efficient on the surface, it misses a critical step: co-creation.

Involving employees from the beginning isn't just about gathering feedback, it's about building ownership. When team members are invited to shape the design, testing, and refinement of automation, they're more likely to understand its value. They can provide on-the-ground insight into where processes break down, which steps are unnecessary, and what outcomes matter most. This doesn't just make the automation smarter, it makes it more relevant, usable, and widely adopted.

Co-creation also humanizes the change process. It signals respect. It shows that leadership trusts its people to help shape the future of how work gets done. This trust strengthens workplace culture and builds a sense of collective momentum. Teams aren't just being told what will happen; they are helping to make it happen. That shift changes everything: attitudes, adoption rates, and even how new ideas are received later down the line.

Of course, co-creation takes time. It requires open forums, discovery sessions, pilot testing, and thoughtful iteration. But the payoff is lasting. Automation becomes something the organization builds together, not something forced on departments by IT or upper management. This collaborative approach doesn't slow progress; it accelerates it by reducing resistance and empowering internal champions who can support their peers through the transition.

True transformation happens when automation becomes a shared vision, not just a strategic directive. And that vision is best built with the people who know the work most intimately.

5.3 Building Digital Confidence Is Just as Important as System Training

Successful automation is not just a matter of installing the right software or defining new workflows. It's also about ensuring that people feel capable, comfortable, and confident using these new systems in their daily routines. The best-designed automation will still underperform if the people interacting with it feel uncertain, overwhelmed, or unsupported. That's why digital confidence must be treated as a core objective in any automation rollout.

Digital confidence goes beyond basic training. It's not enough to run a one-time session and hand out manuals. People build confidence when they are given the space to explore new tools without pressure, the encouragement to ask questions without embarrassment, and the support to try, fail, and try again. This kind of learning culture doesn't just improve system adoption; it boosts morale and future-readiness.

For many employees, especially those who have worked in manual environments for years, automation tools can feel intimidating. They may worry about making mistakes, falling behind, or being judged for not adapting quickly. If these emotions aren't acknowledged and addressed, they create silent resistance. People might follow the new process on paper, but behind the scenes, they'll find ways to default back to familiar, manual routines.

Digital confidence is built gradually, and it requires consistent reinforcement. This can take the form of informal workshops, peer-to-peer learning, dedicated support channels, and real-time troubleshooting. The goal is not perfection, it's progress. Every successful interaction with a new system builds trust in the process. Every moment of clarity strengthens the willingness to embrace further automation.

When digital confidence becomes a shared value across the organization, the effect is visible. Teams begin suggesting new tools, offering automation ideas, and proactively exploring how technology can support their work. They're not just reacting to change; they're co-driving it. And that shift; from cautious users to confident contributors is what transforms automation from a system upgrade into a cultural evolution.

5.4 Automation Should Open Pathways, Not Close Doors

One of the more subtle fears employees often carry, especially during automation transitions, is that their opportunities for growth may shrink. They worry that once tasks are systematized, their roles will become narrower, less necessary, or easier to replace. This fear, though often unspoken, can have serious consequences. It breeds hesitation, self-protection, and ultimately a lack of engagement with the very systems that are supposed to improve performance.

But when approached intentionally, automation can do the opposite, it can expand career paths by eliminating routine work and exposing people to more strategic, creative, and visible contributions. The time saved from automation can be redirected toward higher-level thinking, problem-solving, collaboration, or innovation; skills that are increasingly valuable across all sectors.

Leaders and managers must reframe the narrative. Automation should be presented as a catalyst for professional development, not a ceiling on ambition. When new systems are introduced, so should new growth conversations. Employees should be invited to explore how their roles are evolving, what new responsibilities they can take on, and how the organization is investing in their progression. Whether it's learning new tools, stepping into cross-functional collaboration, or mentoring others, automation creates space for people to grow into roles that are more meaningful and future-proof.

Organizations that embed automation into their learning and development plans unlock even greater value. Upskilling programs, automation-focused projects, and performance reviews that reward adaptability all send a clear message: we're not just replacing tasks, we're building capability. And in doing so, companies position themselves as employers of choice, attracting talent that values growth, curiosity, and long-term impact.

Automation should never feel like an end to opportunity; it should feel like an invitation to more. But that message won't spread by accident. It must be embedded in communication, reflected in leadership behavior, and reinforced through real pathways for advancement. When employees see that automation isn't closing doors, but opening new ones, they walk through them with confidence, not fear.

CHAPTER 6
MEASURING WHAT MATTERS IN AUTOMATION

Automation is not a one-off initiative; it's an ongoing evolution. And like any meaningful transformation, its impact must be measured. Yet many organizations make the mistake of evaluating automation success through surface-level metrics or vague impressions. They count the number of tools implemented or tasks automated, but fail to assess whether those changes actually improved the way the business functions. Without proper measurement, automation risks becoming a series of disconnected efforts rather than a cohesive strategy that delivers measurable value.

The first step in meaningful measurement is clarity of intention. Every automation decision should begin with a clear question: what exactly are we trying to improve? Is it response time? Error rate? Customer satisfaction? Internal workload distribution? Without specific goals, there can be no benchmark for progress. Teams are left assuming things are "better" simply because processes feel faster or systems look cleaner. But speed alone does not equal success. Automation that simply makes a bad process run faster is not progress, it's acceleration in the wrong direction.

Good measurement requires both quantitative and qualitative insight. On the quantitative side, businesses should track clear, relevant metrics: turnaround times, cost savings, task completion accuracy, system uptime, ticket resolution speed, or reduction in manual touchpoints. These indicators show whether automation is working on a technical and operational level. They provide a snapshot of system efficiency. But they don't tell the full story. Qualitative feedback, how employees feel, how customers respond, and how teams collaborate reveals how well the automation fits within the human fabric of the organization. Numbers matter but so does experience.

One of the most overlooked elements of measurement is context. A single metric may look impressive in isolation but lose meaning when considered alongside other factors. For instance, automating a process might cut handling time by half, but if customer satisfaction scores drop because the interaction feels impersonal or inconsistent, the automation is underperforming in a critical area. Likewise, if cost savings are achieved by automating internal workflows, but morale drops due to lack of clarity or support, the long-term sustainability of that automation is at risk.

Automation also needs to be measured in terms of **continuity**. Did the new system create reliance on a single point of failure, or did it distribute ownership and strengthen the process? Did it reduce rework and redundancy over time, or simply shift tasks from one department to another? True success is when automation removes friction across the entire system, not just from one stage of a workflow.

Another important lens is adaptability. Strong automation solutions should evolve as the business grows. Measurement must include not only how well the system works today, but how easily it can be adjusted tomorrow. Does it allow for updates without breaking other functions? Can new steps be added as needed? Is the data it produces helping to inform future decisions? These questions shift automation from being reactive to proactive—from a static solution to a living system that supports agility.

To measure what matters, leadership must also set expectations early. Teams need to understand how automation will be evaluated and how success will be shared. Too often, wins go uncelebrated because no one was tracking the right outcomes. A customer service team that reduced resolution times by 30% through a simple ticketing automation deserves recognition. An HR team that used automation to simplify onboarding and improve new hire satisfaction should be acknowledged. These wins help build momentum, create internal case studies, and shift automation from a background function to a celebrated part of business culture.

Measuring impact also helps prevent automation fatigue. When organizations jump from one automation project to another without pausing to evaluate what worked and what didn't, teams become overwhelmed. They start to see automation as a constant disruption rather than a tool for stability. Regular check-ins, feedback loops, and performance reviews anchored in real data can help avoid this.

Measurement, when done right, acts as a stabilizer. It tells the organization when to accelerate, when to pause, and when to refine.

Organizations should also track adoption rates, not just whether a tool was implemented, but whether it's being used consistently and correctly. Are employees actually logging into the platform? Are workflows being followed as intended? Is there a culture of feedback around the system? High implementation without adoption is a wasted effort. And adoption without improvement is wasted potential. Tracking both ensures that the system is not only in place but performing as intended.

Finally, measurement should drive decision-making. The goal isn't to prove that automation was the right decision, it's to use insights from automation to improve everything else. The data gathered from workflows can reveal opportunities for training, policy changes, product improvements, or customer engagement strategies. When automation becomes a source of intelligence, not just efficiency, it proves its value in ways that go far beyond task automation.

The organizations that succeed with automation are not those that automate the most, they are the ones who measure the right things, refine consistently, and align automation with real business outcomes. They treat measurement not as a final step but as a constant companion to every decision. In doing so, they ensure that automation remains not just active, but effective, always in service of what matters most.

Measuring the effectiveness of automation should not be limited to the weeks following implementation. Often, companies carry out an initial assessment, checking for system uptime, completion rates, or error reductions, and then move on. But automation is not a set-it-and-forget-it solution. Its performance must be tracked consistently across phases of business growth, environmental changes, team transitions, and evolving priorities. What works well today might become a constraint tomorrow if not re-evaluated. This is where measurement becomes not just a metric exercise but a discipline.

Sustainable measurement means building automation performance reviews into operational rhythms. It should be part of regular team check-ins, quarterly reports, annual planning cycles, and executive reviews. Leaders should ask: has this automation continued to save time? Is it still aligned with our team's workflow? Have new pain points emerged as a result of this system? These are not reactive questions, they are forward-looking. They help businesses adapt before bottlenecks grow and ensure that automation evolves alongside organizational strategy.

Equally important is the need to revisit the original purpose behind automation decisions. Was the goal speed, consistency, cost savings, or employee experience? Reassessing whether those objectives have been met without assumptions creates accountability. It also opens up opportunities to correct course, simplify, or even sunset systems that no longer serve their purpose. Not every automation has to stay in place permanently. Some solve temporary problems. Others require restructuring after scale. A culture of active review helps prevent stagnation and over-dependence on systems that are outdated or overengineered.

Organizations must also learn how to adapt their measurement focus over time. In the early stages of automation, metrics may be basic, task duration, error rates, or reduction in manual steps. These are important, but once the initial benefits are achieved, the measurement framework must mature. At that point, more strategic questions emerge. Is automation supporting customer retention? Is it improving decision-making across teams? Is it enabling faster innovation? These are higher-order outcomes that extend beyond the screen and into the very heart of business performance.

There is also an opportunity to track softer, yet equally vital outcomes, such as team satisfaction, perceived workload balance, and confidence in systems. These elements are harder to quantify, but they tell a deeper story. They reveal whether the business is building not just efficient processes, but sustainable environments where people feel empowered. In the long term, this matters more than any percentage point saved in manual work. Because it's people who drive growth and their experience with automation should never be overlooked.

Measurement also fuels iteration. Automation is not static. Once results are gathered, they should inform upgrades, enhancements, or full redesigns where needed. A workflow that works well during low volume periods might need to be optimized under scale. A dashboard that suits one team might not reflect the insights needed by another.

Measurement, then, is not just about proving ROI, it is the feedback loop that shapes the future.

As businesses grow in automation maturity, they should move from tracking only *what* is being automated to examining *how well* automation supports long-term agility. This includes asking questions like: Are we able to quickly test and deploy new automated processes when needed? Are cross-functional teams collaborating around shared performance data? Are we using automation insights to inform strategic pivots or product development? When automation becomes a lens for broader decision-making, its value extends beyond workflows and into leadership itself.

In truth, automation's impact cannot be fully appreciated unless it is consistently observed, questioned, and improved. A strong measurement culture reinforces that automation is not an endpoint, it is an ongoing capability. It evolves with intention. It stays useful because it is assessed with rigor. It delivers real value because it is held accountable not to surface changes, but to strategic contribution.

The businesses that treat automation measurement as a dynamic, living process, not just a compliance task, gain the insight to scale smartly, adapt confidently, and compete with systems that are not only active, but aligned. In such environments, automation doesn't just improve the business, it helps lead it forward.

6.1 Use Data to Empower, Not Control

Automation introduces new visibility into how work gets done. With dashboards, triggers, and real-time logs, businesses can see things they couldn't track before, process duration, task volume, error frequency, and much more. While this level of transparency is useful, it must be used carefully. When automation metrics are weaponized, used to micromanage or punish, trust within teams begins to erode. Employees become defensive, innovation stalls, and people start working for metrics rather than outcomes.

The right way to use data is to empower people with it. Metrics should support teams in seeing where their processes can be smoother, where communication can improve, and where bottlenecks can be removed. They should help individuals understand the impact of their contributions, not surveil them. When automation data is used to encourage ownership and improvement rather than to enforce control, employees begin to view systems as allies, not threats.

For example, a marketing team might use automation data to learn when campaigns are most effective and adjust timing accordingly. A sales team might spot where leads are stalling and refine engagement. A customer support unit might track response time trends and suggest proactive strategies. In these scenarios, teams are not just being evaluated, they are equipped. They're using automation data to refine their own effectiveness.

This shift from top-down reporting to team-centered insight builds maturity. It creates a feedback culture where improvement is shared, not imposed. The data exists to move the organization forward, and when people are given access, context, and support, they start driving that movement themselves.

6.2 Don't Confuse Activity with Impact

One of the biggest risks in automation measurement is mistaking busyness for effectiveness. Organizations often fall into the trap of chasing vanity metrics; numbers that look impressive but don't reflect real value. Counting the number of processes automated or forms digitized is a start, but it doesn't tell you whether those changes actually improved outcomes. Without deeper analysis, teams might celebrate automation for its volume, not its value.

This mindset leads to over-automation, where everything that can be automated is automated, regardless of strategic relevance. Systems get bloated. Employees lose clarity. And the original goal, better performance, gets lost in a blur of disconnected tools and dashboards. That's why businesses must learn to distinguish between activity and impact.

The question is not: how much did we automate? The better question is: **what changed because we automated this?** Did we reduce churn? Did our cycle time improve? Did our customer satisfaction go up? Are our teams spending more time on high-value work? Are decisions being made faster and with better data? These are impact-driven metrics, and they tell the real story of progress.

Avoiding vanity metrics requires a disciplined measurement culture; one that values context over volume and outcomes over optics. It means celebrating quality wins, even when they're small, and questioning broad numbers that don't tie directly to business goals. In the long run, it's this kind of clarity that keeps automation purposeful, lean, and genuinely transformative.

CHAPTER 7
FROM PILOT TO SCALE, MAKING AUTOMATION STICK

I t's one thing to automate a single process or department; it's another to create a scalable, sustainable automation strategy that permeates the organization. Many businesses begin with isolated wins, automating expense tracking, streamlining customer support responses, or integrating a CRM but stop short of expanding these wins into a system-wide shift. The result is a patchwork of disconnected tools and inconsistent workflows. Teams operate in silos. Automation feels like a scattered experiment rather than a unified movement. To unlock the true power of automation, businesses must shift their mindset from one-off pilots to long-term scale.

Scaling automation doesn't mean automating everything at once. It means designing systems that can grow without collapsing. It means establishing a roadmap that links every automation initiative to broader business goals. Too often, businesses become excited by initial gains and rush into large-scale implementation without a strategy. They add more platforms, automate more touchpoints, and launch more initiatives without evaluating how everything connects. This creates fragmentation, drains resources, and erodes trust.

To scale effectively, automation must be rooted in a deep understanding of process flow. Each automation should serve as a building block, not a standalone fix. Once a successful pilot is in place, the next step is to assess its dependencies. What other teams touch this process? What data does it generate or require? How does it fit into the customer journey or internal decision-making cycle? These questions help determine whether the automation can be expanded, refined, or linked to other workflows for greater impact.

Scaling also requires leadership alignment. If only one department or team is invested in automation, its impact will be limited. For real transformation to occur, leadership must view automation as a core strategy, not a side project. This means aligning incentives, dedicating budget, and integrating automation goals into departmental planning. When leaders across departments are working from the same vision, it becomes easier to identify overlapping needs, reduce redundancy, and implement systems that benefit multiple units.

One common barrier to scale is the assumption that all teams must move at the same speed. In reality, automation maturity varies across departments. Some teams are ready to embrace new systems; others may still be refining manual processes or adapting to basic tools. Forcing uniformity often leads to resistance. The better approach is to create flexible pathways for each team, offering phased support and autonomy within a shared framework. That way, automation feels like empowerment, not pressure.

Another crucial factor is documentation. Small automation projects may succeed without detailed records, but as they grow, the lack of documentation becomes a liability. Without clearly defined rules, triggers, ownership, and change logs, teams lose visibility. New hires struggle to understand systems. Updates break existing processes. Scaling without documentation is like building without a blueprint, eventually, the structure buckles. Every automation implemented should come with a clear record of why it was created, how it works, who manages it, and how it fits into the larger ecosystem.

Technology alone cannot ensure scalability. Even with powerful platforms and advanced integrations, automation will stall without culture. Businesses that scale successfully are those that embed automation into how they think, plan, and solve problems. They normalize experimentation. They reward improvement. They invite feedback. In these environments, automation doesn't just come from the top, it bubbles up from every level. Teams feel confident suggesting automations. Employees track their own workflows and propose efficiencies. Cross-functional conversations have become common.

A strong automation culture also knows how to manage change. As systems evolve, people need to be updated, trained, and supported. Communication plays a central role here. Teams need to know what's being changed, why, and how it will affect them. Clear rollouts, support channels, and feedback loops reduce confusion and build confidence. Without this, automation updates become disruptive even if they're technically effective.

Measuring the scalability of automation isn't just about coverage or volume. It's about resilience. Can your systems handle growth, onboarding, seasonality, and new market conditions without requiring constant reinvention? Can your teams adapt to changes in tools without losing performance? Can your processes be updated without breaking everything that surrounds them? These are the true tests of scalable automation, not how much you've implemented, but how easily you can evolve.

Scaling also means knowing when to say no. Not every task needs to be automated. Not every suggestion needs to become a system. Automation at scale requires discipline, a clear line between what drives business value and what creates noise. Businesses that succeed long-term are those that know how to stay focused. They understand that automation is not about quantity, it's about building a smart, interconnected foundation that can grow in any direction without collapsing under its own weight.

7.1 Think Modular, Not Monolithic

One of the major reasons automation initiatives fail at scale is that they're built like giant, all-or-nothing systems. Everything is tightly coupled, rigid, and overly dependent on specific configurations. When one-part breaks, the whole structure stalls. When a change is needed, it disrupts the entire chain. This is a monolithic mindset, and it doesn't hold up well under the pressure of growth.

Modular automation is the smarter approach. It's the idea that each automated process should be designed as a flexible, standalone component that integrates cleanly with others. These components are loosely coupled but strategically connected, making them easier to test, upgrade, and evolve independently. If one module needs to change, it doesn't require rebuilding the whole system. If a new requirement arises, it can be added as an extension rather than forcing a full redesign.

This kind of modular thinking increases resilience. A change in the finance process doesn't have to break something in HR. A tweak to lead generation doesn't risk disrupting customer onboarding. Each part can be improved without compromising others. This reduces risk, simplifies maintenance, and gives teams the autonomy to refine what they own.

It also helps with vendor flexibility. Businesses aren't locked into one software provider or platform. If a better tool becomes available for a specific function, they can switch it out without redoing their entire infrastructure. This kind of agility is essential in fast-moving markets where toolsets change quickly and innovation depends on experimentation, not permanence.

7.2 Turn Automation Knowledge into Institutional Wisdom

As automation becomes part of how the organization functions, it's essential that the knowledge around it doesn't live in silos. Often, automation decisions, why something was set up, what rules it follows, what constraints were considered, live only in the heads of a few people. If they leave, change roles, or become unavailable, that knowledge disappears with them. What's left behind is a functioning system with no context, making it difficult to improve, troubleshoot, or build upon.

Organizations must prioritize turning automation knowledge into institutional wisdom. This means documenting not just *what* was automated, but *why*, *how*, and *with what implications*. It means capturing lessons learned during implementation: what worked, what didn't, what would be done differently. These insights are gold, not just for future automations, but for onboarding new team members, avoiding repeated mistakes, and informing broader strategy.

Creating a shared knowledge base, through wikis, internal playbooks, or collaborative tools ensures that automation becomes part of the organization's learning culture. It signals that improvement isn't just a technical exercise, it's something that should be understood, refined, and shared across departments.

Over time, this kind of transparency builds an organizational memory. Teams don't have to reinvent the wheel. New hires don't feel lost in fragmented systems. Leaders can make informed decisions based on patterns rather than isolated examples. Automation, in this sense, evolves from a string of processes into a growing body of insight that strengthens the business at every level.

CHAPTER 8
CHOOSING THE RIGHT PROBLEMS TO SOLVE

The value of automation lies not in how much a business can automate, but in what it chooses to automate. At the heart of every successful initiative is a clear, well-defined problem worth solving. Yet, too many automation projects are driven by trends, peer pressure, or vendor pitches rather than a careful understanding of internal needs. Without strategic focus, automation can become a collection of disconnected efforts, busy, expensive, and ultimately disappointing.

The smartest organizations start by identifying friction points that slow the business down or compromise quality. These are not always the most obvious or technical. Sometimes, it's a five-minute task repeated a hundred times a day. Sometimes, it's the manual approval step that delays decisions. Sometimes, it's the customer inquiry that falls through the cracks. Automation is most effective when it removes pain that is deeply felt but poorly addressed.

This requires observation; quiet, intentional observation. Leaders and teams need to watch how work actually flows, not just how it's described in handbooks or dashboards. They need to ask hard questions: Where do we see delays? What consumes time but adds little value? What mistakes keep happening? What tasks could be completed without a human decision? Automation is not about replacing people; it's about removing friction that prevents people from doing their best work.

When businesses don't start with the right problem, they end up automating processes that don't need to exist in the first place. They digitize clutter. They lock bad habits into software. They create workflows that are efficient but still irrelevant. In these cases, automation becomes a source of complexity instead of clarity. That's why the first step should never be the tool, it should always be why.

Another reason businesses miss the mark is that they confuse volume with impact. A process repeated thousands of times may seem like the best candidate for automation. But if it only saves seconds and contributes little to strategic outcomes, it's a shallow win. In contrast, automating a lower-frequency task, like compliance checks or customer handoffs might unlock greater long-term value by improving accuracy, reducing risk, or enhancing customer experience.

The right problems are often those that sit at the intersection of cost, complexity, and strategic importance. Automating these types of problems doesn't just make life easier, it improves how the business performs. It strengthens the company's reputation, increases employee satisfaction, and removes operational drag that holds back growth. In other words, solving the right problems with automation delivers results that ripple outward, touching more than the immediate workflow.

Another common pitfall is trying to solve too much at once. Automation doesn't need to address the entire business on day one. In fact, trying to automate everything too quickly usually leads to shallow implementation and poor adoption. The better approach is to focus on one valuable, well-understood problem at a time. Solve it fully. Learn from it. Then expand. This builds momentum, sharpens understanding, and improves the quality of each new rollout.

What's also important is choosing problems that align with your business's current maturity. A startup might focus on automating lead generation, because growth is the primary focus. A scaling business might target internal approval flows, where bottlenecks start to appear. A mature enterprise might invest in automating compliance, audit readiness, or advanced forecasting. The right problem to solve is not universal, it's contextual. It's about knowing where your business is now and what's getting in its way.

Customer-facing problems also deserve priority. Delays in support, inconsistent onboarding experiences, or missed follow-ups often hurt brand trust. Automating parts of the customer journey, without losing the human touch can dramatically improve retention and satisfaction. But again, the key is focus. Automating every customer interaction at once can feel cold or disconnected. Start with the moments that matter most, the ones that create lasting impressions or where breakdowns happen often.

When organizations build their automation roadmap around the right problems, they build credibility. Teams see that automation isn't about chasing trends, it's about solving real issues. Confidence grows. Buy-in improves. Adoption increases. And most importantly, automation becomes a source of strategic strength, not just a technical convenience.

In the end, automation is only as valuable as the problems it is applied to. The goal isn't to digitize everything. It's to remove the blocks that slow people down, frustrate customers, or create avoidable cost. That clarity, knowing what matters and starting there is what separates automation that sticks from automation that distracts.

8.1 Look for What Repeats, Even When It Seems Small

Some of the most valuable automation wins are hidden in the repetitive, seemingly minor tasks that fly under the radar. These are the everyday activities that take just a few minutes at a time, logging updates, confirming receipts, sending reminders, organizing data, transferring files. On their own, these tasks appear too insignificant to warrant a full automation effort. But their frequency is where the opportunity lies.

What happens once or twice a day may not feel disruptive. But what happens twenty, fifty, or a hundred times a week quickly becomes a silent productivity drain. Multiply that across teams and time zones, and the impact becomes more serious than expected. These micro-processes quietly erode creative energy, delay high-value work, and force talented people to spend their best hours on routine maintenance.

When teams are encouraged to track these patterns, they often uncover surprising sources of inefficiency. A manual client onboarding email. A routine invoice review. A repeated search for files or forms. These are precisely the kinds of problems automation excels at solving. And because they're small and clearly defined, they're often easier to automate, test, and improve.

By starting with what repeats, businesses gain quick wins. They reduce cognitive overload and reclaim time without disrupting core operations. More importantly, they build confidence. Each successful automation, no matter how small, reinforces the mindset that not everything has to be manual. The result is a culture of continuous improvement, where teams begin to notice inefficiencies as opportunities rather than inconveniences.

8.2 Don't Just Patch, Design for Enduring Value

Another trap businesses fall into when choosing problems to automate is defaulting to short-term fixes. They look for pain points, apply a quick automation, and move on. While this may bring immediate relief, it often leads to a string of disconnected solutions that require constant maintenance and offer limited long-term impact. Automation becomes a patchwork, not a platform.

This is particularly common in fast-paced environments where speed is prized over strategy. But shortcuts in design eventually cost more, financially, operationally, and culturally. A tool that isn't scalable will need to be replaced. A workflow that doesn't integrate across teams will cause confusion. A process that hasn't been evaluated end-to-end might just shift the problem elsewhere.

Sustainable automation starts by asking: "If we solve this now, will it still serve us six months or a year from now?" That doesn't mean every automation has to be enterprise-grade. But it does mean that even simple fixes should be approached with clarity and care. Is the logic clean? Is the ownership clear? Is it built on a stable foundation, or are we just plugging holes?

When businesses commit to solving the right problems the right way, they create systems that can grow with them. They avoid rebuilding the same solutions multiple times. They increase trust in their tools. And they train teams to think beyond urgency, to think in terms of resilience, scalability, and strategic alignment. That shift in thinking changes the game: from reactive patchwork to a forward-looking, automation-powered business.

CHAPTER 9
LEADERSHIP IN AN AUTOMATED ENVIRONMENT

As automation becomes embedded into the way businesses operate, leadership must evolve with it. The nature of decision-making, delegation, oversight, and team dynamics changes when systems take on more of the operational load. In this environment, leaders are no longer just task managers or department heads, they become architects of direction, alignment, and adaptability. Their role is not diminished by automation; it is refined and elevated.

In a manual world, leadership often involves tracking who's doing what, ensuring deadlines are met, and catching errors before they grow. But automation absorbs many of those responsibilities. It handles reminders, approvals, notifications, and even complex data flows. This shifts the leadership focus away from constant supervision and toward strategic foresight. Leaders must now ask different questions: Are our systems aligned with our goals? Do our teams have what they need to make informed, independent decisions? Are we building a structure that scales without bottlenecks?

Leadership in an automated environment is about empowering teams, not micromanaging processes. When the system handles routine execution, human time becomes more valuable—and leadership must protect and guide that time. Rather than chasing deliverables, leaders should spend more energy building clarity, removing blockers, and fostering creative problem-solving. The most effective leaders are those who use automation not as a replacement for people, but as a platform that enhances team contribution.

But this transition isn't automatic. It requires a deliberate mindset shift. Many leaders are accustomed to equating visibility with control. Without constant updates, status meetings, and manual oversight, they may feel disconnected. Automation can make it seem like things are happening "in the background" and for some, that's uncomfortable. Trust becomes essential. Leaders must develop the ability to lead through outcomes, not presence. They must trust the systems they've put in place, the people they've trained, and the indicators they've chosen to monitor.

This also means learning how to interpret new kinds of information. Automated environments generate data, lots of it. But data without context is noise. Leaders must develop fluency in automation dashboards, system reports, and workflow analytics, not just to track performance, but to spot emerging trends and risks. Data literacy has become a leadership skill. And more than just understanding the numbers, leaders need to ask: what are we learning from this data?

What decisions can it support? Where are the blind spots it doesn't capture?

A key part of leading in this environment is building shared ownership of automation. While technical teams may lead implementation, the systems that are created touch every part of the business. Leaders across functions, sales, finance, HR, operations must understand their role in guiding, supporting, and continuously improving automated processes. This calls for collaboration, not competition. It requires leaders to engage beyond their own silos, to ask how their department's automation links to others, and how joint processes can be refined for mutual benefit.

The tone set by leadership also influences how automation is perceived throughout the organization. If leaders frame automation as a way to eliminate roles or cut corners, teams will respond with fear or resistance. If they frame it as a way to free up time, increase focus, and elevate human contribution, teams will lean in with curiosity and support. In this way, automation is not just a technical decision, it is a cultural one. Leaders are the translators between what automation does and what it means for the people it touches.

Great leadership in an automated environment also includes creating a safe space for learning and iteration. Not every automation will work perfectly. Some will need refining. Others will require rollback or replacement. Instead of hiding these moments, strong leaders treat them as opportunities for growth. They normalize testing, celebrate lessons learned, and avoid punishing early failures. This culture of experimentation is vital for long-term success. It turns automation from a rigid structure into a living system that evolves with the business.

As automation systems become more embedded, one of the greatest responsibilities of leadership is maintaining emotional awareness. It's easy to focus on metrics and overlook the emotional impact that change, especially repeated, technology-driven change can have on individuals. Even positive automation outcomes like reduced workload or better structure can trigger discomfort if the emotional terrain isn't managed well. Employees may feel uncertain about their value, disconnected from their previous identity, or anxious about being left behind.

This is where emotional intelligence becomes not just useful, but essential. Leaders who listen actively notice resistance early and respond with empathy help build a psychologically safe environment; one where teams feel comfortable asking questions, giving feedback, or expressing doubts without fear of judgment. Automation may streamline processes, but it's human-centered leadership that preserves trust through those transitions. The most effective leaders in automated workplaces are not just technically informed, they are emotionally present.

Another key role of leadership is maintaining visibility without reverting to micromanagement. One of the paradoxes of automation is that it removes many of the traditional checkpoints' leaders are used to, manual reports, status updates, and visible daily routines. In their absence, some leaders overcorrect by inserting new layers of oversight or demanding excessive reporting from automated systems. This only creates noise and undercuts the autonomy that automation is meant to provide.

Instead, leaders must embrace strategic visibility. This means knowing where to look, what to monitor, and when to step in without disrupting flow. It means trusting the automation to surface exceptions, risks, or anomalies and trusting the team to respond before escalation is required. This level of visibility is built on well-designed metrics, clear communication, and a shared understanding of goals, not on hovering over every action. It's less about watching everything, and more about designing systems that surface what matters.

As automation spreads, leaders also become the stewards of narrative continuity. In periods of change, employees look to leadership not just for answers, but for meaning. Why are we doing this? Where are we headed? How does my role evolve in this environment? Without clear communication, the gaps left by these questions are filled with speculation, doubt, or resistance. But when leaders communicate consistently and contextually, they help teams anchor themselves, even as processes evolve around them.

This communication shouldn't be reserved for formal meetings or milestone updates. It should be integrated into the culture of the organization. Informal check-ins, visual dashboards, strategy roundtables, and open retrospectives all give leaders opportunities to reinforce the broader story: that automation is not replacing contribution, it's refining it. That change is not a threat, it's a tool. And that each person's role in that story still matters deeply.

It's also vital that leaders lead, by example, in learning and adapting. When employees see their managers embracing new tools, asking smart questions, and owning their own growth curve, they are more likely to do the same. But when leaders exempt themselves from automation, or show reluctance to evolve, it sends a signal that growth is optional, or worse, avoidable. In high-performing environments, leadership isn't just about direction, it's about participation. When everyone, including top management, shows up with a learning mindset, automation becomes a shared pursuit, not a top-down mandate.

The modern leader in an automated workplace is a strategist, an enabler, a communicator, and a learner. They don't need to code the systems themselves, but they need to understand what those systems do, how they impact people, and where they create opportunity. They lead not by enforcing control, but by curating clarity. Not by dictating action, but by designing space for better action to happen.

Above all, leaders must remember that automation doesn't absolve them of responsibility, it expands it. With manual complexity reduced, the human complexity comes into sharper focus: managing motivation, building trust, resolving conflict, and aligning purpose. These are not tasks that can be automated, and they never will be. They require attention, reflection, and leadership with depth.

As businesses accelerate their automation journeys, the presence of calm, emotionally intelligent, and future-oriented leaders will be one of the biggest differentiators between companies that automate successfully and those that simply install systems.

9.1 Creating Automation Champions Within Teams

One of the most scalable things a leader can do in an automated environment is decentralize influence. Rather than becoming the sole driver of automation efforts, effective leaders identify, support, and elevate automation champions within each team. These are individuals who are curious about systems, quick to adapt, and naturally collaborative. They may not have formal authority, but they hold deep influence through trust, initiative, and credibility.

These champions serve as a bridge between leaders44444hip vision and day-to-day execution. They help explain why changes are happening, encourage others to try new systems, and offer honest feedback on what's working or not. When empowered, they reduce the burden on managers and create a layer of grassroots momentum that leadership alone cannot sustain.

Building this internal network starts by observing, not assigning. Leaders should look for individuals already taking the initiative to streamline tasks, who ask thoughtful questions in meetings, or who naturally assist others during transitions. Once identified, these champions should be given the space, recognition, and tools to lead quietly but powerfully from within. This distributed model of leadership reinforces that automation is not a top-down command, it's a culture everyone contributes to.

9.2 Leading Through Uncertainty, Not Just Efficiency

While automation is often associated with clarity and predictability, its implementation is rarely neat. New systems bring temporary confusion. Established habits are disrupted. Outcomes might be delayed. This creates an environment of **uncertainty**, which, if unmanaged, can trigger fear, frustration, and disengagement.

This is where true leadership is tested. Leading through uncertainty requires composure and transparency. It means acknowledging that discomfort is part of the process, not pretending everything is under control. Leaders who are honest about unknowns and who share the plan for moving through them build far more trust than those who try to spin every challenge as a win.

Uncertainty also presents a rare opportunity: it invites teams to learn how to solve problems in real time, together. Leaders can use these moments to teach adaptability, model calm under pressure, and invite diverse thinking. Rather than rushing to resolve ambiguity, strong leaders help their teams sit with it just long enough to find better answers.

In a world where systems do much of the repetitive work, it's these human responses to complexity that set resilient organizations apart.

Automation may stabilize the technical landscape, but it's leadership that stabilizes the emotional and cultural one.

9.3 Balancing System Dependence with Human Judgment

As automation becomes more sophisticated, the risk of over-reliance on it increases. Leaders may be tempted to trust dashboards over people, or automated decisions over human input. While systems are built for consistency, it's human judgment that ensures relevance, context, and nuance remain intact.

An over-automated mindset can lead to rigidity. It treats processes as unbreakable, even when reality calls for flexibility. Leaders must create space for exception handling, for discretionary thinking, and for conversations that override the system when necessary. This doesn't weaken automation; it strengthens it by keeping it responsive to the real world.

Equally, leaders must teach teams when to lean on the system and when to step outside it. This requires communication, scenario planning, and often, case-by-case calibration. If automation is the engine, human judgment is the steering wheel. Both must work in harmony.

When leaders model this balance by knowing when to follow the process and when to question it, they create organizations that are both efficient and thoughtful. Businesses that not only move fast but move wisely.

CHAPTER 10
SUSTAINING THE AUTOMATION MINDSET

The true success of automation lies not in its launch, but in its longevity. While it's tempting to view automation as a project with a finish line, the reality is that it functions more like an operating philosophy, a way of seeing and shaping work that must evolve with the business itself. Sustaining automation is not about building bigger systems. It's about nurturing the mindset that brought automation into the organization in the first place: one rooted in clarity, curiosity, and continuous improvement.

Over time, automation that once felt innovative will begin to feel routine. Processes will settle. Tools will become familiar. And if not carefully managed, the organization can drift into complacency. Leaders stop questioning workflows. Teams work around systems instead of refining them. Improvements are made reactively, only when something breaks. When this happens, the automation mindset begins to fade, not because it failed, but because it was never actively maintained.

To avoid this, businesses must treat automation as a dynamic ecosystem. Just like products evolve, so must process. Regular reviews should be built into operations, not as audits, but as discovery sessions. Where is time still being lost? What steps feel redundant? What feedback have we been ignoring? These questions keep automation alive. They ensure that the system continues to serve people, not the other way around.

Another part of sustaining automation is staying open to new possibilities. As tools advance, integrations become smoother, and AI capabilities expand, the range of what's possible increases. But none of that matters if the organization is mentally stuck. A sustainable automation culture is one that experiments without fear. It pilots new features, evaluates new tools, and encourages team members to suggest improvements. Innovation is not isolated in a tech team; it becomes part of how the organization breathes.

Sustainability also depends on systems being easy to update and accessible to those who need them. Overengineered automation often becomes fragile. If only one person understands how a process was built, the business becomes vulnerable. But when systems are documented, modular, and transparent, others can learn, refine, and extend them. This not only protects the organization, but it also empowers it.

What sustains automation more than anything, however, is relevance. If a process no longer supports the way the team works, it needs to be revised or removed. Automation should never be preserved out of nostalgia or sunk costs. It should be evaluated based on whether it's helping the business work better right now. Systems that are no longer served must be retired without hesitation. Otherwise, automation becomes bureaucracy: rigid, outdated, and counterproductive.

The automation mindset also needs champions, people at every level who continue to ask, "Can this be done better?" These aren't just technical specialists. They are project managers, marketers, analysts, HR officers, and customer service reps. Anyone who interacts with systems regularly is in a position to notice what's working and what could improve. A sustainable automation culture listens to those voices. It creates channels for feedback and rewards people for spotting opportunities.

Sustainability isn't about keeping everything running. It's about keeping the right things running and being willing to rebuild when needed. It's about knowing that automation isn't a one-time fix, but a long-term commitment to doing better work in better ways. The goal is not perfection. The goal is progress that doesn't stall.

In the end, automation is less about technology than it is about mindset. It is about choosing to question instead of conforming. It is about improving without being prompted. It is about designing systems that support the real work, not distract me from it. And it is about building an organization where clarity, flow, and forward motion are not the result of pressure but the natural rhythm of how things are done.

Those who embrace this mindset don't just automate. They evolve. They stay sharp. They stay relevant. And in a world where change is constant, that is the truest advantage any business can have.

Sustaining the automation mindset requires intentional reinforcement from leadership. Over time, as systems stabilize and the initial excitement fades, the enthusiasm for automation can quietly erode unless it's nurtured. Leaders play a pivotal role in keeping the vision alive, not through constant campaigns or dramatic changes, but through consistent signals. When a team lead integrates process reflection into regular standups, when a department head encourages workflow reviews quarterly, or when a CEO publicly credits automation for an operational breakthrough, those acts compound. They reinforce the culture silently but powerfully.

This long-term consistency also depends on how success is recognized. Early on, teams may be motivated by tangible time savings or reduced errors. But over time, these wins become normalized, and new incentives must emerge. Sustained motivation often comes from recognition, not just of outcomes, but of initiative. When someone improves a system, identifies a better way to automate a manual task, or removes friction for a customer, that effort should be visible. A culture that celebrates thoughtful automation, not just speed, is more likely to keep improving.

But automation isn't sustained by leadership alone. The teams closest to the systems must feel empowered to co-own the journey. This means avoiding centralization that stifles change. If every improvement request has to pass through multiple layers of approval, progress will stall. A truly mature automation culture gives teams enough autonomy to optimize their own workflows, with support, yes, but without bureaucratic hurdles. It creates space for trial and error, for small wins to be tested and scaled, and for feedback to be seen not as complaint but as insight.

Documentation remains one of the most important, and often neglected, tools for long-term sustainability. Automation built without records becomes legacy faster than expected. New team members can't understand it. Those who maintain it become gatekeepers, whether they want to or not. Over time, the system's flexibility weakens. But when organizations build with transparency, logging what has changed, why, and how, it creates a resource that outlasts individuals. It ensures automation is not dependent on memory, but on shared intelligence.

Future-proofing automation also requires a deliberate approach to tool selection. Businesses must resist the temptation to chase hype. Every tool added to the ecosystem should have a clear reason for existing, linked to a real problem, a measurable outcome, and an integration plan that won't compromise what's already working. Switching platforms for novelty or popularity creates disruption and confusion. Instead, long-term automation thrives on tools that can evolve, not tools that create lock-in.

As environments shift, due to regulation, technology trends, customer behavior, or even global events, the systems you've built will need to flex. The automation mindset doesn't cling to the past. It is adaptive by nature. It welcomes review, invites adjustment, and sees change not as a disruption but as a natural progression. Organizations that succeed long-term don't just protect what works, they prepare to rebuild better when necessary.

The final thread in sustaining automation is mindset mentorship. Senior staff who've gone through automation transitions must share their experiences. Not just the successes, but the hesitations, the missteps, and the learning curves. This kind of storytelling builds organizational wisdom. It creates a safety net for those who are newer to the process, and it preserves hard-earned insights that can be lost in silence. Automation, when passed down as a living practice, becomes a part of the company's DNA.

And that's where the shift becomes permanent. Automation is no longer a program. It's no longer a project. It's not something you *do*, it's how you *think*. It's how you evaluate work. How you challenge inefficiencies. How you decide whether effort should be manual or repeatable. It becomes a lens. A filter. A philosophy.

The businesses that survive, more importantly, the ones that will lead, are those that don't stop integration. They don't stop implementation. They live the mindset. They refine, they question, they upgrade not just their systems but their thinking. And that's what makes the difference between automation as a feature and automation as a future.

10.1 Treat Automation as a Living System, not a Fixed Asset

One of the biggest reasons automation initiatives stagnate is because they're treated like assets to be installed and left alone. A workflow is automated, the system runs, and teams move on, until something breaks or no longer fits. But automation is not a one-time deployment. It's a living system that exists within a dynamic business environment. As conditions change, new regulations, customer needs, team structures, and technology, automation must also evolve.

Treating automation as a living system means planning for its maintenance, adaptation, and reinvention from the start. Just as buildings require upkeep, automation systems need ongoing care. Logic should be reviewed periodically. Permissions should be updated. Redundant automations should be removed. New opportunities should be explored as systems mature, and data reveals fresh inefficiencies.

When automation is managed like something static, it quickly becomes a liability. But when it's treated like something alive; something to observe, update, and improve—it becomes a reliable part of the organization's growth strategy. It's no longer a project with an end date. It's a continuous resource that supports better decisions, stronger execution, and faster learning.

This shift in treatment; from static to living, requires new habits. Calendar moments for review. Cross-functional audits. Team reflections on what's working and what isn't. The businesses that embed these practices make automation an active contributor to evolution, not just a quiet piece of infrastructure in the background.

10.2 Preserve the Human Experience as You Automate

In the drive for efficiency, it's easy to forget that behind every automated system are people, using it, reacting to it, relying on it. The purpose of automation isn't to strip work of its humanity but to remove friction so humans can focus on deeper, more valuable tasks. When automation is done well, it doesn't erase the human experience; it amplifies it.

Sustaining the automation mindset means continuously checking in on how people feel about the systems they're using. Is it intuitive? Is it supportive? Does it reduce stress or create new types of frustration? Automation should not just save time; it should improve the quality of that time. Systems should feel helpful, not heavy. Clear, not confusing. When they do, engagement increases. When they don't, even the most technically flawless automation risks becoming underused or bypassed.

This mindset also means recognizing the emotional dynamics of automation. Some team members may feel insecure as systems take over what used to be their responsibilities. Others may feel overwhelmed by the speed of change, or the learning curve involved. These are not side issues; they're core to sustainability. A team that feels seen, supported, and respected in an automation journey is far more likely to sustain and optimize it long-term.

Leaders and designers alike must prioritize usability and empathy. Every automated workflow, every dashboard, every notification should be designed with the user in mind. Does it give clarity or create confusion? Does it align with the user's rhythm, or does it interrupt it? The automation mindset is not anti-human, it is pro-clarity, pro-capacity, and pro-collaboration.

When people feel that automation helps them do their best work; not just faster, but smarter and with less stress, they're far more likely to keep improving it. That's how systems stay relevant. That's how the culture of intelligent automation sustains itself from the inside out.

10.3 Design for Resilience, Not Just Performance

Many automation efforts focus exclusively on speed and precision. Can we reduce time? Can we eliminate errors? Can we increase throughput? While these are valuable outcomes, they only paint part of the picture. Systems built for performance but not **resilience** are fragile. They work well under perfect conditions, but struggle the moment something changes, fails, or scales beyond the original plan.

Sustaining automation requires thinking beyond best-case scenarios. It requires planning for what happens when things go wrong. What if a step in the process fails? What if a data source changes? What if an integration times out or a policy update shifts a compliance rule? Without resilience built into the system, through alerts, fallback options, clear ownership, and documented recovery steps, even minor disruptions can create major consequences.

Resilience also applies to the people managing the systems. If automation is centralized in the hands of a few technical experts, the business becomes vulnerable. When those individuals leave or get overwhelmed, the system slows or stops. Sustainable automation distributes knowledge, builds cross-functional fluency, and ensures no single person is a bottleneck.

A resilient automation culture also includes buffer space; time and flexibility for teams to review, reflect, and adapt. When systems are constantly pushed to the limit with no room for pause or adjustment, even small cracks eventually widen. But when teams are given time to recalibrate, they can keep the system healthy and responsive, ready not just for today's challenges, but for tomorrow's surprises.

Resilience is what allows automation to stay relevant in unpredictable conditions. Businesses that prioritize it will be the ones that not only survive change but absorb it, adapt, and come out stronger on the other side.

10.4 Keep Learning Alive Across the Organization

Automation maturity isn't just about systems; it's about people continuously growing with those systems. If learning stops, so does progress. Yet many organizations treat automation training as a one-time event: onboard the team, run a few tutorials, and assume everyone is set for life. But as tools evolve, workflows change, and strategies shift, knowledge must evolve too. Without a culture of continuous learning, automation becomes outdated, even if it's technically still running.

Sustaining the automation mindset means making learning a living part of the organization. This doesn't have to mean formal training sessions every month. It can be as simple as open demos of new tools, team retrospectives that highlight lessons learned, or weekly check-ins where improvements are shared. When learning becomes embedded in the rhythm of work, it feels natural. It becomes part of how people contribute, not an extra task, but a core behavior.

This culture must extend across every level. Leadership should model curiosity, not just about strategy, but about systems. Mid-level managers should champion shared learning between departments. And frontline staff should be encouraged to ask questions, suggest improvements, and build confidence in their ability to engage with automation tools. No one should feel that automation is "someone else's job." Ownership grows when people are informed, empowered, and included.

Continuous learning also closes the loop between adoption and adaptation. When teams are learning consistently, they don't just use systems, they improve them. They understand why a process was built a certain way, and they feel equipped to question or refine it when it no longer fits. That agility, driven by informed teams, is what keeps automation from becoming stale or burdensome over time.

Organizations that build learning into their automation DNA will outlast those that rely solely on technical implementation. Because in the long run, it's not just systems that drive performance. It's people, learning, sharing, and leading the change together.

REVIEWS

1. Temidayo Ogunlana

Head of Business Operations, Veritrax Logistics, Ibadan

"What Taiwo presents in *Sync or Sink* isn't hype, it's clarity. For years, we've focused on growth without fully addressing the cracks in our operations. This book helped us recognize that without structure; scale is just a ticking clock. I wish I had this perspective five years ago."

2. Ifeanyi Agbazue

Co-founder, PriceMile.ng (E-commerce platform), Enugu

"I've read plenty of books on digital transformation, but few speak directly to businesses like ours, still growing, still figuring it out. His language is direct, and his mindset around automation isn't just technical, it's strategic. *Sync or Sink* gave me new language for conversations I've been struggling to lead with my team.

3. Sa'adatu Garba

Software Solutions Analyst, Yola Finserve Technologies

"This is not just a business book; it's a systems-thinking guide. I was particularly impressed by how Taiwo weaves in technical understanding without overwhelming the reader. It's now a part of our internal reading list for all new hires in the engineering team."

4. Uduak Etim

People and Process Consultant, Calabar

"We work with a lot of traditional businesses undergoing digital transformation. Many of them are skeptical about automation. *Sync or Sink* makes the case with empathy, structure, and experience. It's going straight into our client resource kit."

5. Babajide Omoleye

Strategy Lead, Elevare Advisory Partners, Lagos

"Every chapter in this book is actionable. Taiwo doesn't just ask leaders to automate, he shows them how to think about it properly. His insights into systems, people, and workflows are sharp and real. This book will stay on my desk, not my shelf.

REFERENCES

Accenture. (2022). *Human + machine: Reimagining work in the age of AI.* https://www.accenture.com

Atlassian. (2021). *Automation in agile teams: Case studies and tools that deliver.* https://www.atlassian.com/blog

Bain & Company. (2023). *From pilots to full scale: Accelerating automation adoption in large enterprises.* https://www.bain.com

Deloitte. (2023). *Automation with intelligence: Pursuing organization-wide reimagination.* Deloitte Insights. https://www2.deloitte.com

Forrester Research. (2021). *The future of work: Intelligent automation will shape the enterprise workforce.* https://www.forrester.com

Gartner. (2023). *Hyper automation: Beyond robotic process automation.* https://www.gartner.com

Godin, S. (2018). *This is marketing: You can't be seen until you learn to see.* Portfolio/Penguin.

Harvard Business Review. (2020). *Reskilling in the age of automation.* https://hbr.org

IBM Institute for Business Value. (2022). *Rethinking work: The role of automation and AI in shaping the future workforce.* https://www.ibm.com/thought-leadership

McKinsey & Company. (2022). *The state of AI in 2022 and a half decade in review.* https://www.mckinsey.com

MIT Sloan Management Review. (2022). *Digital transformation and leadership in automation projects.* https://sloanreview.mit.edu

Ries, E. (2011). *The lean startup: How today's entrepreneurs use continuous innovation to create radically successful businesses.* Crown Business.

Toyota Motor Corporation. (n.d.). *Kaizen: The philosophy of continuous improvement.* Adapted from the Toyota Production System.

World Economic Forum. (2023). *The future of jobs report 2023.* https://www.weforum.org/reports/the-future-of-jobs-report-2023

Omisogbon, T. (2017–2024). *Personal field notes & implementation logs from enterprise automation consulting projects.* [Unpublished internal documentation].